KU-449-028

JOHN HODGE

Collaborators

faber and faber

First published in 2011
by Faber and Faber Limited
74–77 Great Russell Street, London WC1B 3DA

Typeset by Country Setting, Kingsdown, Kent CT14 8ES
Printed and bound by CPI Group (UK) Ltd, Croydon, CR0 4YY

With thanks to Ruby Films, Film4 and Miramax

The right of John Hodge to be identified as author
of this work has been asserted in accordance with Section 77
of the Copyright, Designs and Patents Act 1988

A CIP record for this book
is available from the British Library

ISBN 978-0-571-28399-6

2 4 6 8 10 9 7 5 3 1

Acknowledgements

In 2007, I was commissioned to write a screenplay about the wild youth of the Georgian bandit/revolutionary Joseph Dzughashvili, better known by the name he later adopted: Stalin. The principal source for this was to be Simon Sebag-Montefiore's *Young Stalin*, a vivid and wonderful account of the tyrant's early years. The director (of the proposed film) and I went through the book in search of a story. There is no shortage of incident in Stalin's early life (and no shortage of myth either), but we struggled to find the narrative – the beginning, middle and end that would make for a satisfying screenplay. As with the life of any major historical figure, there was a temptation to cram too much into our story, or else we found a frustrating inconsistency in the behaviour of the subject. If only these people would lead their lives with subsequent film adaptation in mind, the life of screenwriters would be so much easier.

Our attention then settled upon a footnote in Simon's book. It described the attempt, in 1938, by Mikhail Bulgakov, to write a play on the very same subject, the youth of Stalin. I must admit I knew very little about Bulgakov, but after reading several of his plays and novels, and learning at the same time more about the events of 1937–38 in the Soviet Union, the whole episode struck me as fascinating. At the height of the terror, while millions of innocent men and women were being arrested for their supposed crimes against the regime, here was a man quite clearly (on the basis of his work) opposed to Bolshevism being awarded (or sort of volunteering for) the job of dramatising his oppressor's youth. At last, we felt, we had found our story. I wrote a script. The producers were polite.

The financiers said nothing. Where, I think they wondered, were the bank raids that feature in the biography? The serial seductions also? Where, indeed, was Young Stalin? I offered to start all over again, and at the time of writing I'm still at it, but now in a format more suited – six hours of television. Meanwhile, the director left, with the parting observation that perhaps I should turn the first version into a play.

So here it is.

May I thank the following without whom, one way or another, it would not have happened: Pawel Pawlikowski, Simon Sebag-Montefiore, Alison Owen, Hannah Farrell, Paul Trijbits, Tessa Ross, Billy Hinshelwood, Anthony Jones, Sebastian Born, Nick Hytner, and some men whom I have never met but to whose works of history and biography I am indebted: Robert Conquest, Donald Rayfield, Robert Service, Lesley Milne, and the late Michael Glenny for his translations of Bulgakov's plays.

Introduction

There is a passage in Robert Conquest's brilliant, monumental epic *The Great Terror* where the insane brutality of the process he recounts now seems to infect the prose: 'The Deputy Commissar for Justice was severely criticised in January and shot.'

It is as though the author, overwhelmed, has given up on any attempt to identify due legal process, any fragment of justification for execution, just as they were abandoned in Stalin's Soviet Union. The reader too adapts to this new logic and it is a shock, when you stop to think, to realise that you are no longer surprised. *Why, if a man is criticised in January, then of course he will later be shot.*

Welcome to Moscow, 1938. It is in this atmosphere, in fact this deadly reality, that Mikhail Bulgakov, aged forty-seven, will undertake his most hazardous assignment, and how often – in all honesty – can you say that about a playwright?

Here we join him, a novelist and librettist as well, looking for a theatre to take his work. The stage adaptation of his own novel *The White Guard* has been a huge success, running at the prestigious Moscow Art Theatre for over eight hundred performances. The success, however, is tainted. He was forced to change the ending (the story of White Russians living in Kiev during the turmoil of the civil war) to make it politically acceptable. Of his other plays, *Flight* (also featuring White Russians as heroes) is banned, as are *Last Days* (Pushkin's battle with the Tsar Nicholas I), *Madam Zoyka* (a satire on Lenin's New Economic Policy), and *Molière* (the playwright's extinction at the court of Louis XIV). This last one hurt especially.

By now, Bulgakov is an author in distress. The artistic and commercial success of *The White Guard* keeps him afloat, but the horizon is empty and his future looks bleak. At an emotional low, he writes privately of his intention to give up the theatre. It is into this gloomy domestic scene that a new opportunity is delivered. Bygones are to be bygones, censorship lifted and the pariah readmitted, for it turns out that the stage needs him as much as he needs the stage.

The MAT has a privileged status, the double-edged gift of Stalin. It has been allowed a tour to Paris with the actors waved through customs on their way home. Its senior figures have travelled to Germany for medical treatment, but are not denounced and tried as spies on their return. In exchange for these favours, the company is supposed to showcase all that is great in Soviet drama. There is only one problem: Soviet drama is dismal. There is propaganda, of course, no shortage of work written to the Bolshevik order, but the MAT is supposed to be above all that. They need quality *and* ideological rectitude, Marxist orthodoxy with a human twist, a big bold hit that doesn't get anyone in trouble. So they turn to the man they know is in need of a break, a man with talent, a man who has previously toyed with the dangerous notion that they now present to him late one night in his cramped, cold apartment.

They want him to write a play about Stalin. In return, he asks for a new apartment. An agreement is reached. A deal is done.

But Bulgakov, I believe, had no choice but to deliver the play he eventually did. People well known to him and his wife, Yelena, had been arrested. The poet and playwright, Vladimir Mayakovsky was driven to suicide (or possibly assassinated). Another poet, Osip Mandelstam died for, basically, writing a poem. Actor and theatrical innovator Vsevolod Meyerhold was banned, arrested and eventually shot, so the first actor to shoot the seagull was himself shot on the orders of the man who wore the seagull badge (the MAT's gift to its all-powerful sponsor). The terror was in full swing: show trials, hysteria, fear and paranoia were the background to daily life. And even with all that, if Bulgakov had been exceptionally brave (or foolhardy) on his own account, he had to think of his wife. An act of rebellion or refusal would have doomed Yelena too, perhaps before him. In a surviving document from the NKVD, four categories for arrest are listed. The first three are various definitions of enemies of the people. The fourth is quite simply: 'wife'.

If he had good reasons not to decline the challenge, it is also likely that he actively wanted it. I don't think it is a conjecture too far to suggest that Bulgakov felt he had some sort of relationship with the man who ruled the Soviet empire. Like Molière before him, he had come to the attention of the supreme ruler and found himself now utterly dependent on the indulgence of that ruler for his continuing ability to work and to live. For Stalin had taken a liking to *The White Guard* and had seen the play many times. He had even attended with his old comrade and fellow member of the Politburo Sergei Kirov in November 1934, only two days before Kirov was murdered (probably, as it happens, on Stalin's orders). But four years before that, the paths of playwright and tyrant had already crossed. In 1930, in despair and anger, the victim of a campaign of persecution and believing he had no future in the USSR, Bulgakov had applied for permission to emigrate. Stalin, in one of his characteristically Olympian interventions (a surprise phone call from the Kremlin), threw Bulgakov a lifeline, the promise of work at the MAT.

It was the first act in a near decade-long tease that would lead, in the end, to a telegram, a train journey interrupted and the damning faint praise of the ultimate critic. Stalin had given Bulgakov hope, a gift in its own way more destructive than despair. In the years that followed that call, his work approached production but never quite got there (*Molière* was rehearsed nearly three hundred times). Bulgakov was driven to distraction, torn between feeling saved and knowing he was doomed. He longed for a message from above, a signal to tell him where he stood. But in the years that followed, there was none.

Bulgakov should not have been surprised. One of Stalin's most effective tactics was the use of uncertainty: a subtle alteration in job description might lead to arrest weeks later. Or, just possibly, it might not. Criticism and apparent reprieve washed over Party officials like waves tossing their victims one way then the other while the tide dragged them slowly further from the shore. False reassurance and broken promises were a matter of policy at the highest level. Even after death, a deliberate fog persisted. Thousands sentenced to 'ten years [of imprisonment] without right of correspondence' were in fact secretly executed – their loved ones' flickering hope for the future nothing more than a cruel illusion. In limbo, Bulgakov was far from alone.

So giving in to, or being inspired by, the idea of writing a play about Stalin, must have seemed like a way to send a message 'upstairs', to provoke a response, one that would at last tell Bulgakov: saved or doomed?

For whatever reasons, then, he accepted the commission and he did what anyone might do: he attempted to reconcile the conflicting, contradictory impulses. On the one hand, he must not write anything critical of or hostile to Stalin. There are bullets waiting for men who do that. On the other, he is at heart a believer in the freedom of the individual, a humane liberal, a satirist, and his craft is crying out to be used. Surely these two cannot be married. But he tries. And, perhaps thrilled to be working again, to feel the old juices flowing, he believes that he has succeeded. Yelena records that readings of scenes to friends were met with enthusiasm. Here he is, it seems, taking on the biggest subject available, the single outstanding feature of life in this nation, the object of its cult – its leader – and, he feels, making a decent fist of it.

And meanwhile the terror reaches full strength, a bewildering torrent of arrests, confessions trials, and punishments. Day and night, the meat-grinder does not pause. The Gulag swells with human fodder. Mass graves are dug and filled. Philatelists, engineers, students of Esperanto, artists, peasants, army officers, railwaymen, foreigners, factory workers, Party officials, all fall into its maw. The instrument of terror, the NKVD itself, is not spared: several thousand of its officers are shot. The terror becomes, in the phrase of Robert Service, 'systematically arbitrary'. Pretence of finding actual perpetrators of actual crimes is replaced with a more direct approach. *Prikaz*, operational orders, simply instruct the functionaries across the USSR to round up a certain number of people who fit the bill and deal with them accordingly. There are no punishments for exceeding your quota but a shortfall is fatal.

To dabble in numbers here is to enter an arena of controversy and partiality. In an online world, we can all find whatever estimates suit our own point of view. Nevertheless, it seems reasonable to give credence to those scholars who have been to the trouble of actually researching the primary evidence (i.e., proper historians) and in turn to give the most credence to those proper historians who are most cited by other people who have researched the primary evidence (i.e., other proper historians). What else can you do? Most of us weren't actually there. But, allowing for the above, a useful place to start may be the comment in Nikita Khrushchev's memoirs: 'Ten million or more of our citizens paid with their lives in Stalin's jails and camps.'

And then, in November 1938, with surprising rapidity, it fizzled out, this paroxysm of savagery. Perhaps it had been unsustainable: by this time, it has been reported, nearly half the urban population was on a list that should lead to arrest. Or perhaps it had simply served its purpose: all resistance to Stalin is broken, the populace is cowed, and the Party and institutions of state have been made anew. Until his death, there will be no challenge to the authority of the *Vozhd*.

So the terror tails off (though it never disappears) and in a flourish of chutzpah Stalin manages to blame it all on someone else: his head of the NKVD, Nikolai Yezhov. They even give the whole episode a name, the *Yezhovshchina*. The man himself is appointed Commissar for Water Transport, which must have seemed like a death sentence. If it didn't, it should have. A few months later, his successor at the organ of state security, Lavrenti Beria, has Yezhov arrested and shot, then strolls round to present Stalin with a list of a few hundred friends and family of poor old Nikolai whom he now seeks approval to liquidate. So it goes.

And Bulgakov has made progress. He is ill now, dying of the same kidney disease that killed his father, but he works on and the producers are pleased with what they read. In good spirits, he and Yelena set off with designers and directors from the MAT to do research in Stalin's home, the Soviet Republic of Georgia. They never get there. They are recalled by a telegram ('journey unnecessary'), and the creative process is at an end.

What are we to make of the result of all this, the play Bulgakov entitled *Batum*? (After the Black Sea oil town where the action takes place.)

It is, I would say, a pale imitation of his other work. How could it be otherwise? His head was not free to think, his hand not free to write. His other plays have zest and humanity, often what feels like spontaneity, at some moments as though the work has been casually thrown together. If that leads to some passages being less sure-footed than others, then it only reminds us that the author is a human rather than a Soviet machine. But there is none of this in *Batum*. The humour is forced, the drama is linear and predictable, and the leading character (you know who) is a synthetic goody two-shoes, a boring Marxist who never sets a foot wrong but who somehow inspires and leads the dullards around him. The romance is cursory and simplistic (in contrast with the authentically complicated affairs in *The White Guard*, *Molière* and *Last Days*). In *Batum*, only the authority figures have any depth, but even they feel like emasculated reproductions of his previous villains. Bulgakov did what he was compelled to do: he sacrificed a quantum of his own credibility to sanitise and glorify the despot.

It was all for nothing. Stalin, an assiduous reader and theatregoer, took pity on his favourite playwright. For him too, there were conflicting impulses: on the one hand, he was tempted by the prospect of a play by Bulgakov, but on the other, a tyrant must take care of his image. In the words of Service again, Stalin 'could kill artists at will, but he knew that his policies could only produce great art if he overlooked, at least to some extent, what the artists were really doing'.

Perhaps, like Bulgakov, Stalin hoped that the two impulses could be reconciled, and if so, he can only have been disappointed in the result. The play was submitted for approval and his verdict was returned: *Batum*, he decided, was 'a very good play . . . but not to be staged'. Bulgakov had delivered the play that, in a better world, he would never have written and now, for better or for worse, it would never be performed.

From *Molière*, Act Four: 'All my life I've licked his spurs and thought of only one thing – don't crush me. And now he has crushed me all the same. The tyrant!'

Bulgakov never did get the apartment. His supporters, perhaps trying to shield him from judgement, have combed the text of *Batum* to find hidden messages of rebellion.

Well, fair enough, they may be there if you hold it up to the light and tilt it a certain way. For myself, I am not convinced, but I don't think it matters one way or the other. I may have taken the liberty of renaming his play and subjecting it to parody, but I intend no criticism of the man. There is no need to shield Bulgakov from anything. The tyrant cornered him and toyed with him for his own pleasure. When it was over, there was time left for nothing but the end.

Or almost nothing. In the last months of his life, Bulgakov completed *The Master and Margarita*, his novel in which the Devil visits Moscow. So with this parting shot he added to what he had already created: an outstanding body of work, in drama and in prose, an incredible achievement under the most extreme of circumstances. In 1938, he was a brave man trying to survive, both literally and artistically, and if *Batum* does not live up to his own standards, then what of it? For Mikhail Bulgakov, a true hero of the Soviet Union, owes nobody an apology.

JH, September 2011

Collaborators was first performed in the Cottesloe auditorium of the National Theatre, London, on 25 October 2011. The cast was as follows:

Mikhail Bulgakov Alex Jennings
Yelena Jacqueline Defferary
Joseph Stalin Simon Russell Beale
Vassily Patrick Godfrey
Praskovya Maggie Service
Sergei Pierce Reid
Grigory William Postlethwaite
Anna Jess Murphy
Vladimir Mark Addy
Stepan Marcus Cunningham
Doctor Nick Sampson
Actor 1 Perri Snowdon
Actor 2 Michael Jenn
Eva Sarah Annis

Other parts played by members of the company

Director Nicholas Hytner
Designer Bob Crowley
Lighting Designer Jon Clark
Music George Fenton
Sound Designer Paul Arditti

Characters

Mikhail Bulgakov
a writer, aged forty-seven

Yelena
his wife, thirty-something.

Vasilly
ex-aristo, sixty-something,

Praskovya
a teacher

Sergei
a young man

Grigory
a young writer

Anna
an actress

Vladimir
an NKVD officer

Stepan
an NKVD officer

Doctor

Two Actors

Man, Woman, Eva, Nurse, Two NKVD Men, Driver, Cleaner, Doctors, Apothecaries, Molière, Lagrange

and

Joseph Stalin
a dictator, aged fifty-nine

COLLABORATORS

Act One

One double bed.
   One large table, two chairs.
   Typewriter, decanter, and two glasses on table.
   Telephone on a wooden stand.
   Gramophone on a wooden stand.
   One large cupboard/wardrobe with double sliding
doors.

As the curtain rises, it is night.
   Bulgakov is lying asleep.
   Beside him on the bed is Yelena, also sleeping.
   All is quiet.
   Then there is a knocking sound. Soft at first but soon
loud.
   A rhythmic regular thumping.
   Bulgakov awakes.
   He shakes his wife but she does not stir.
   He gets out of bed.
   He searches for the source of the noise.
   It grows louder and faster.
   Eventually, he realises: the knocking comes from
within the cupboard.
   He approaches. Stands in front of the door.
   The knocking reaches a coda, and with a final thump,
it stops.
   Cautiously, Bulgakov raises a hand to the door.
   And suddenly the door slides violently open.
   A backlit silhouetted figure inside lets out a yell.
   Bulgakov jumps back with a shriek.
   The figure jumps out.
   He is Joseph Stalin.

Music starts: a silent-movie funny-chase tune.
Stalin pounces towards Bulgakov.
Bulgakov flees.
Stalin, slightly comedic – a malicious Groucho Marx –
follows suit.
Stalin pursues Bulgakov around the room and over
the bed.
A chase around the table.
Around and over the bed again.
Back to the table.
Stalin picks up the typewriter.
He swings it at Bulgakov.
Bulgakov evades but trips.
He lies on the floor.
He looks up to Stalin looming over him with the
heavy typewriter.
Stalin mugs to the audience – 'Will I or won't I?'
Stalin brings the typewriter down with a vicious sneer.
Blackout.

Lights up. Dawn.
Mikhail Bulgakov is sitting on the side of his bed.
Head in his hands, breathing deeply.
A hand falls on his shoulder.
He turns to face Yelena.

Yelena Did he catch you?

Bulgakov No. No, he didn't. I was too quick for him.
Grabbed the typewriter, jammed his fingers in and typed
'You bastard' all across his knuckles.

Bulgakov begins to dress.

Yelena That's a good sign. Did you have your clothes
on?

Bulgakov I think so.

Yelena Did he?

Bulgakov Why? Do you secretly fantasise about your husband in a naked love romp with the General Secretary of the Central Committee of the All-Union Communist Party of the Union of Soviet Socialist Republics?

Yelena I just wondered if he was hairy.

Bulgakov He probably is, but I think it's illegal to know.

Bulgakov kisses her on the cheek.
She looks at him with concern.

Yelena How do you feel?

Bulgakov Fine. I feel fine. I mean just the same. It's nerves, Yelena. Anxiety. That'll be the diagnosis.

He kisses her again.
Enter Praskovya and Vasilly, who sit at the table.
Bulgakov pulls on his jacket and crosses towards them.

Vasilly Good morning, Bulgakov!

Bulgakov Good morning, Vasilly, Praskovya.

Praskovya Good morning, Mr Bulgakov. How are you this morning?

Bulgakov I'm fine, thanks.

Praskovya But you look ill. An immediate and unassailable contradiction, I think.

Bulgakov No, really, I'm fine.

Praskovya You've lost weight. Your colour is poor. You have bad dreams.

Bulgakov No, I don't.

Praskovya Did he catch you this time?

Bulgakov We are not going to talk about my dreams –

Praskovya He caught you.

Bulgakov No.

Praskovya He always catches you. There is no escape from him.

Bulgakov Praskovya, I am grateful for your concern.

Vasilly Coffee, Mikhail?

Bulgakov We have coffee?

Vasilly No. Of course not. I am simply uttering words of desire at random.

Bulgakov Large cup, please.

Vasilly And let's see what else.

    He slides opens the empty cupboard.

Look! Fresh fruit! Salami! Pickled vegetables!

    He slides the door shut.

Bulgakov Nothing for me, thanks.

Praskovya You see. He's not eating.

Bulgakov Only because there's nothing to eat.

Vasilly Tell, me Mikhail, did you enjoy a hot bath this morning?

Bulgakov Vasilly – I forgot!

Vasilly So did I! Like the fool I am, I made do with a few drops of cold water rubbed vigorously into the creases of my dusty skin. I wouldn't say it was enjoyable, but I was glad when it was over.

Praskovya Like life itself.

Vasilly Praskovya – teaching history, don't you find that difficult? I mean, what do you do when your pupils ask what life was like in the old days?

Praskovya I tell them –

Vasilly You tell them!

Praskovya I tell them – it's in the textbooks.

Vasilly But what if they say, 'No, Madame, tell us what you remember'?

Praskovya I remember nothing.

Vasilly But you must remember something, Madame!

Praskovya Quite the opposite: it is imperative that I remember nothing, that no one remembers anything, and you would do well to remember that.

Vasilly Oh, but I can't forget. You know something, Mikhail –

Bulgakov Your peasants loved you.

Vasilly My peasants loved me. I know you lefty liberals don't like to hear that sort of thing, but it's true. Oh yes, it was a system founded on oppression – I mean their grandfathers were serfs to my grandfather – and their well-being was entirely dependent on my benevolence – but at least I was benevolent.

Bulgakov No one starved on your estate.

Vasilly No one starved on my estate!

The cupboard door slides violently open.
A young man in fatigues steps out.

Sergei That is treason!

Praskovya and Vasilly are unperturbed.

7

Bulgakov Who is this?

Sergei Sergei Rastolnovich, Comrade. Shock Worker in the Red October engine factory.

Bulgakov And what is he doing in our kitchen cupboard?

Praskovya Assigned by the housing committee.

Bulgakov Our apartment is full. Two bedrooms barely worthy of the name. Vasilly sleeps in the cupboard in the hall! Are we now to have an adolescent where there ought to be tinned apricots?

Vasilly Tinned apricots! Please – Bulgakov!

Praskovya We all have to make sacrifices.

Sergei Only through personal sacrifice can we maintain the strength of the motherland. Personal sacrifice in the Soviet Union is a matter of honour and pride.

Vasilly You'll fit in very well here. Coffee?

Enter Yelena.
   She is dressed to go out and carries Bulgakov's coat.

Ah, Madame Bulgakov, good morning! I have saved you two slices of yesterday's bread and a small lump of something that might or might not be . . .

Yelena Thank you, Vasilly. I shall share it with my husband.

Praskovya He was caught last night. That's a bad sign.

Yelena Good morning, Praskovya.

Bulgakov Meet Sergei. The new boy.

Yelena Delighted to meet you, Sergei. I hope you're very happy here.

Sergei Comrade Madame Bulgakov – it is a great honour to be living in the depths of your cupboard.

Vasilly I'd stop there, young fellow. This man uses words for a living: a metaphor like that could lead you into all sorts of trouble.

Enter the Doctor. Dirty white coat, unshaven. He carries a stack of files under one arm, and a bag containing stethoscope, sphygmomanometer, etc. He stands at the edge of the stage.

Doctor Next!

Yelena hands Bulgakov his coat.

Yelena Misha – we'd better go.

Bulgakov Yes, of course.

He pulls his coat on.

Vasilly Well, good luck, old man.

He shakes Bulgakov's hand. Praskovya kisses Yelena.

Praskovya I hope for the best. Though I fear for the worst.

Doctor Next! Come on!

Sergei The motherland will clutch you to its bosom and restore you with the milk of its kindness, issuing forth in limitless bounty –

Vasilly coughs. Sergei stops. Vasilly points into the cupboard. Sergei withdraws. Vasilly slides the door shut.

Doctor I have fifty patients to see this morning!

Bulgakov (*to Vasilly and Praskovya*) Don't worry. I'm sure it's nothing.

Vasilly takes Praskovya's arm and they walk away.

Praskovya Did you see? He didn't eat his breakfast.

She and Vasilly exit.
Bulgakov sits at the table.
Yelena stands behind him.
The Doctor strides across.

Yelena Good morning, Doctor.

Doctor Name.

Bulgakov Bulgakov. Mikhail.

Doctor The playwright?

Bulgakov Yes.

Doctor I saw one of your shows once. A woman responds to the economic woes of post-revolutionary Russia by establishing a bordello in a cramped Moscow apartment.

Bulgakov *Madame Zoyka.*

Doctor There was, at one point, as I recall, a more or less naked woman upon stage.

Bulgakov There may have been.

Doctor I disapproved. The following night, I disapproved more strongly still. And on the third night, now taking my place in the front row of the stalls, well, you can imagine –

Bulgakov The full extent of your disapproval.

Doctor We made eye contact. She smiled. At me.

Yelena Doctor, my husband is very ill.

Bulgakov It's just nerves, I think.

Doctor Still working – is she?

Bulgakov Sorry?

Doctor That actress.

Bulgakov I believe so. I'm not sure where.

Doctor But you could find out. Could you?

Yelena He's losing weight. He feels sick. He won't eat. He's tired all the time.

Doctor You could tell her that I'm a doctor, that I'm single, or at least I am for all practical purposes, and that I have my own –

He taps them.

Bulgakov Dentures?

Doctor Teeth.

Yelena Doctor. Please.

The Doctor sighs. Stands and walks around to Bulgakov.

Doctor Mouth.

Bulgakov opens wide.

Ah.

Bulgakov Aaaah . . .

He shines a torch in Bulgakov's eyes.

Doctor Sleep?

Bulgakov Yes.

Yelena No. He doesn't.

Bulgakov Badly . . . Only sometimes.

The Doctor prods his abdomen.

Doctor Pain?

Bulgakov No.

And harder.

Yes!

The Doctor wraps the sphyg cuff around Bulgakov's arm –

Doctor I'll never forget her . . . smile.

– and measures his blood pressure.

And are you aware of a tinge in your skin, a pigmentation?

Bulgakov No.

Yelena What does it mean? Please understand – my husband trained – as a doctor.

Bulgakov A long time ago.

Doctor What sort?

Bulgakov Venereologist.

Doctor A strange choice, I always think.

Bulgakov Someone has to do it.

Doctor Like writing plays! Tell me – have you ever used morphine? Personally, I mean.

Bulgakov Why?

Doctor Why not? A lot of doctors do. Stress. Fatigue. Loneliness. You wouldn't be the first, I can tell you.

Yelena That's all in the past.

Doctor Of course. Ever had high blood pressure before?

Bulgakov No.

Yelena Is it high now?

Doctor Now please – your arm.

Then he produces what he needs from his bag.
He ties a tourniquet around Bulgakov's arm.
Enter a man in seventeenth-century French costume.
This is Molière.
The Doctor screws a needle on to his glass syringe.
He starts to take blood from Bulgakov.
Enter a Chorus of grotesque masked Doctors and
Apothecaries brandishing huge syringes and knives.
The comic awarding of a diploma.

Chorus *Bene, bene, bene, respondere / Dignus est intrare /*
in nostro corpore . . .

Molière *Clisterum donare / Postea bleedare /* afterwards
. . . purgare.

Chorus *Bene, bene, bene, respondere / Dignus est intrare /*
in nostro corpore . . .

Molière collapses. He cries out, staggers, and falls.

Molière Help me! Help me!

He falls on to the bed and dies.
The Doctor has completed the taking of blood from
Bulgakov.

Doctor Come back next week. And if you do happen to
bump into that actress . . .

He taps his teeth.

Yelena Doctor –

Doctor Good day, Madame!

Exit the Doctor.

Another masked character, Lagrange, steps forward from the Chorus.

Lagrange This day, while playing the role of Argon, Molière has collapsed on stage and was taken, unshriven, by the relentless hand of death. For this I shall mark the day with a black cross. What was the cause of it? Why did it happen? How shall I put it? The reason for this was the King's disfavour.

The sound of applause and cheering.
Enter Grigory, clapping and cheering.
Molière, the Chorus, Lagrange pull off masks.
Then they cross to meet Bulgakov and Yelena.
Grigory joins them. He greets one of the actors, Anna, with a kiss.
The mood is celebratory. Mutual congratulation. Champagne is produced.
Enter Vladimir and Stepan. They saunter on, conspicuous but unnoticed in their hats and black leather greatcoats.
Vladimir sits at the table.
Stepan stands back.
They watch the celebrating thespians impassively.

Yelena Misha – they loved it!

Bulgakov Do you think?

Yelena Yes! Of course. It's been worth it, Misha, it's all been worth it.

Bulgakov Everyone was great. You were wonderful! To my cast!

Anna To Mikhail!

Bulgakov To *Molière*!

Grigory To the King!

Bulgakov To autocracy!

Grigory Tyranny!

Bulgakov Tyranny without redress. Where would we be without it?

The joke is appreciated. All toast and the party continues.
   Grigory approaches Bulgakov.

Grigory Well done, Mikhail.

Bulgakov Thanks, Grigory. Glad you enjoyed it.

Grigory It's a statement. Man versus monster.

Bulgakov And the monster wins.

Grigory But the man never gives in. He dies true to his own beliefs.

Bulgakov That's what they don't like. They'd sooner you lived than you died free in your own mind.

Grigory Well, they won't like what I've got for them then.

Bulgakov Your novel?

Grigory I've submitted it.

Bulgakov Be careful now! They'll come back to you: listen, Comrade, this can be published, but you must make some changes, you must extol the virtues of our glorious leaders, display the unlimited happiness and sincere gratitude of the masses, and so on . . . But you take no notice.

Grigory I stand my ground.

Bulgakov You wait. You change nothing. You re-submit. If necessary, you re-submit again. You get there, in the end.

Anna approaches.

Anna The party's moving on –

Grigory Mikhail?

Yelena It's been a long day.

Bulgakov Yelena's right. I'm old, I'm tired, I'll only slow you down.

Yelena and Bulgakov make their goodbyes.
Grigory, Anna, the Chorus, etc., all exit.
Vladimir and Stepan still watch.
The lights fade and Yelena and Bulgakov meander towards the bed in moonlight.

Yelena I enjoyed it.

Bulgakov Really?

Yelena Of course. I'd tell you if I didn't.

Bulgakov Would you?

Yelena Yes. I would. I mean not right now, obviously. But . . . eventually.

Bulgakov You are my most honest critic.

Yelena And the only one you sleep with. I hope.

They pass the cupboard.
Bulgakov opens it up.

Bulgakov Goodnight, Sergei!

Sergei (*from within*) Goodnight, Comrades Mr and Mrs Bulgakov!

Bulgakov slides the door shut.
He and Yelena reach the bed.
Yelena drops her coat and pulls off Bulgakov's.
Slowly, she pulls him to the bed.

Yelena I'm a dictator. I may force you to do certain things.

They lie down in embrace.
Vladimir and Stepan stand up.

Lights fade up slightly. Dawn.
Stepan knocks hard against the table. And again.
Yelena wakes, jumps up and forward, just as Sergei
emerges from his cupboard.
Vladimir and Stepan approach.

Yelena Good morning –

Vladimir Good morning to you, Madame. We're looking for a Mr Mikhail Bulgakov.

Yelena May I say who's calling?

Bulgakov approaches.

Bulgakov What do you want?

Vladimir We're here to arrest you!

Yelena Oh my God!

Vladimir Only joking! I love that one. Always gets a reaction. You must be Yelena. It's a pleasure to meet you. I'm Vladimir, this is Stepan. NKVD.

He addresses Bulgakov.

We want to talk to you. In private.

Bulgakov I have no secrets –

Vladimir – from my wife. That's what every man says. But you'd be surprised. Madame, would you excuse us?

Yelena stays where she is.

Madame?

Yelena This is my home. My husband. I'm staying exactly where I am.

Vladimir Please. Otherwise I'll have to make my little joke again. Only this time it won't be funny.

Sergei Comrade Madame Bulgakov, perhaps you would care to play chess in my room?

Yelena Why, yes, Sergei, I would be delighted.

She kisses Bulgakov on the cheek and goes into the cupboard.
Sergei follows.

Vladimir That's your room?

Sergei It's my cupboard. Well, actually, it's Comrade Madame Bulgakov's cupboard.

Vladimir That's enough of that!

He slides the door firmly shut.

You approve?

Bulgakov He's a sweet kid.

Vladimir Bohemians. Wouldn't happen in my house. What a shitty apartment. How many people do you share with?

Bulgakov We share with three others.

Vladimir But you write a lot of letters, complaining – don't you?

Bulgakov says nothing.

Yeah. You never give up.

Bulgakov What do you want?

Vladimir We saw the play. Very moving. Molière – playwright, satirist, thorn in the flesh of an oppressive regime – he dies on stage! How fitting. How tragic.

Bulgakov It's based on truth.

Vladimir Of course. And is that your dream, Mr Playwright? To emulate your hero. To be a thorn in the flesh of an oppressive regime. To die on stage.

Bulgakov I have no wish to die anywhere.

Vladimir Good sense. But you know – you're a lucky guy. That you're not in prison is a miracle. Tell me: when you went to Istanbul, did you meet Trotsky?

Bulgakov I have never been to Istanbul.

Vladimir Always difficult to prove a negative.

Bulgakov In fact, as I'm sure you're aware, I have never left the Soviet Union.

Vladimir Not for want of thinking about it, eh, Comrade? You write a lot of letters.

Bulgakov Yes.

Vladimir You never give up.

Bulgakov Is that a crime?

Vladimir Oh, yes! Wonderful! How I love the steamy indignation of a righteous liberal! Go on, tell me, please: it's like living in a police state.

Bulgakov Are you here to arrest me?

Vladimir You're a clever guy. But treating us like fools is not clever. Do you think we can't see what the play is about?

Bulgakov As I say –

Vladimir – it's based on truth. How long have you been working on it?

Bulgakov On and off . . . difficult to say, really.

Vladimir Of course, I appreciate that. But in rehearsal, I mean, how long?

Bulgakov Well, the play's been scheduled and cancelled so many times –

Vladimir How long?

Bulgakov I don't remember.

Vladimir Three years. Two hundred and ninety-six rehearsals in three years.

Bulgakov As many as that?

Vladimir And then – at last – finally – we have the opening night! Must be an incredible experience, after all that time and effort, all that emotional commitment, to finally see it realised upon the stage, and to hear it received with such warmth, such genuine enthusiasm. What an amazing feeling. Like the release of years of tension, the reward for years of hope.

Bulgakov Something like that.

Vladimir Well, treasure the memory, sucker, because the first night was also the last.

He lets it sink in.

Now come with us.

Bulgakov I'll just tell my wife.

Vladimir No. Come with us.

They walk away.
The cupboard door slides open.
Sergei and Yelena look out.

Sergei Don't worry, Comrade Madame Bulgakov – I do not believe they will execute him without the formality of a fair trial.

He pulls the door shut.
Vladimir walks and talks with Bulgakov.

Stepan lurks behind.

Vladimir Stalin's date of birth?

Bulgakov Twenty-first December 1878.

Vladimir Good citizen! So, in celebration of his forthcoming sixtieth birthday, what you're going to do – what we respectfully invite you to do – is to write a play about the early life of our great leader, Joseph Visarionovich Dzughashvili, a.k.a. The Vohzhd. It's going to be a surprise!

Bulgakov I think you want someone else.

Vladimir Not at all! We want you. You know, you're actually one of his favourites. You wrote that one about the family in Kiev.

Bulgakov *The White Guard.*

Vladimir *The White Guard*! He's seen it. Fifteen times. That's how much he likes you. Fifteen! I saw it myself. Counter-revolutionary bullshit, if you ask me. I mean, the heroes are Tsarists – how does that work?

Bulgakov They convert to Bolshevism.

Vladimir Oh sure. In the end, they convert. But you can tell their heart isn't in it. Just like I can tell the playwright's heart wasn't in it. But what do I know? The General Secretary likes your style. That's why you've been chosen as his birthday surprise.

Bulgakov I cannot write a play about Stalin!

Vladimir Why not?

Bulgakov I have just been informed that my work is banned!

Vladimir I know. I was there. I spoke the words.

Bulgakov Don't you realise what that means to me?

Vladimir Yes. A gap in your schedule.

Bulgakov I'm finished. That is what it means.

Vladimir You'll get over it! You are a skilled dramatist. What you are going to give us is . . . The Truth.

Bulgakov is deadpan.

Here we are.

Bulgakov The Lubyanka?

Vladimir Relax, you're not going into the prison. I have an office here. You can borrow it.

Bulgakov Why would I want to do that?

Vladimir Because you can't work in that shitty apartment.

He leads Bulgakov to the table and chairs.
Stepan follows.

So what do you think? If there's anything you need, you can let me know.

Vladimir is about to leave.

Bulgakov Stop! Hold on. You think I'm going to do this? Because I can tell you right now that I am not going to do this!

Vladimir You're not?

Bulgakov No.

Vladimir Right. Well, that's my plan ruined. What an idiot I am! You see, I hadn't made any provision for you expressing your free will. Don't suppose you'll change your mind?

Bulgakov No.

Vladimir Please?

Bulgakov No!

Vladimir What if I was to offer you something?

Bulgakov There is nothing you could offer me. Except a ride home.

Vladimir Oh but there is! Isn't there? Let's think about it. You write this play for our leader's sixtieth birthday and in return, your *Molière* can be performed again.

Bulgakov says nothing.

Yes, that's it. You write for us: *Molière* goes back on, your career is salvaged, you get another chance, Bulgakov, indeed you may even have a future, which is no minor consideration in this day and age. But if you say no, I mean if you don't write for us: it's all over.

Bulgakov How would I . . . know I can trust you?

Vladimir Sir, I think you've spent too long in the world of show business. Here in the Secret Police, a man's word is his bond.

He extends a hand to shake.
Bulgakov does not move.

Your last play took three years. We have four weeks. I suggest you get moving.

Exit Vladimir and Stepan.
Bulgakov remains at the table.
Enter Yelena, Anna and Grigory.

Grigory You're not going to do it, are you?

Bulgakov Of course not.

Grigory You told them that?

Bulgakov I made it clear.

23

Anna It's a punishment, that's what it is. For daring to think.

Yelena But it's not easy, is it?

Grigory You think he should do it?

Yelena No . . . I'm not saying that. But his play, what happens to that?

Bulgakov As Sergei would say, we all have to make sacrifices.

Yelena And all the other people who've worked on it?

Anna Even if he does what they ask, who's to say it would ever see the light of day again?

Yelena He gave his word.

Grigory A secret policeman, please!

Bulgakov Grigory's right . . . I have to take a stand. I have to . . . it is my obligation . . .

He gets up. Turns away in thought.
Grigory follows him. Interrupts. A talk in private.

Grigory Mikhail – I need your advice.

Bulgakov What?

Grigory My novel.

Bulgakov What? Rejected?

Grigory No. Banned. I'm not allowed to publish it anywhere. Nor show it to anyone. I've been ordered to destroy it.

Bulgakov Don't do that. No, not that, whatever you do.

Grigory They've suggested I 'restructure' myself. They say my next novel should be about the defence of the motherland, or the reform of some counter-revolutionary who sees the light through the purifying effects of digging a canal. Apparently there's quite a market for novels about counter-revolutionaries who see the light through the purifying effects of digging a canal. It's a genre in itself, I never even knew –

Bulgakov Meet them eye to eye. Do not blink, do not step back. Change not one single word.

Grigory That's what I wanted to hear.

Bulgakov Good luck.

Grigory And you.

> *They shake hands. Grigory exits with Anna.*
> *Yelena watches Bulgakov, who stands in silence.*

Yelena What are you going to do?

> *He turns to her. They look at one another. She knows. She comforts him with a hug.*
> *They part. As Yelena exits, Bulgakov turns to the table and sits down.*
> *He feeds paper into the typewriter.*
> *But he does not type.*
> *Enter Vladimir and Stepan.*
> *Vladimir shouts across.*

Vladimir Bulgakov? Are you writing?

Bulgakov I'm thinking.

Vladimir I can't hear anything!

Bulgakov It's a silent process.

Vladimir I want to hear the sound of creation.

Bulgakov When you stop pestering me, you'll hear this!

> *He brusquely types a couple of words.*

Vladimir That's better. What have you written?

Bulgakov 'Death to Stalin!'

Vladimir and Stepan stride across.
Vladimir spools out the page. Reads it and tears it up.

Vladimir Bulgakov – is there something wrong?

Bulgakov No.

Vladimir Are you sure? With your health or something? I wouldn't want to think I've hired a man who isn't up to the job. I don't like to be personal, but there's a kind of tinge in your skin – have you noticed that? Maybe all writers have got it.

Bulgakov It's the colour of persecution.

Vladimir So the problem is just a creative one, right?

Bulgakov There is no problem. It's all coming together in my mind.

Vladimir Good. Then when can I see something on the page?

Bulgakov A day or two. At the most.

Vladimir OK. A day or two. At the most, Bulgakov. At the most.

Exit Vladimir and Stepan.
Bulgakov sits.
Enter Yelena. She stands behind Bulgakov.
Enter the Doctor carrying a large bundle of files.

Doctor Next! Sit down. Seventy-five patients to see! What is the nature of your problem?

Bulgakov We're here for the results. Of the tests.

Doctor Name.

Bulgakov Bulgakov. Mikhail.

Doctor Smackhead groin doc turned smut-scribe?

Bulgakov That's me.

Doctor How could I forget?

He reaches for a file.

Well?

Bulgakov What?

Doctor Any joy?

Bulgakov I'm sorry?

Doctor The actress. The babe. The honey. The hot chick. *Mia amorata.* Have you found her yet?

Bulgakov I'm working on it.

Doctor You'll let me know. I'll never forget her . . . smile.

Bulgakov Do you have my results?

Doctor All right!

He snatches a file and reads.

Let's see . . . Fifteen letters, eighth letter 'c', anagram of 'censorship loser'.

Yelena What!

Doctor Progressive failure of the kidneys, hypertension, declining filtration rate –

Bulgakov Nephrosclerosis.

Doctor You *were* a doctor!

Yelena Is it bad? Mikhail?

Doctor Will you tell her or will I?

Bulgakov Things get worse.

Doctor That's one way of describing it.

Bulgakov The loss of appetite, and weight, continue. And the sickness. Then one starts to retain fluid, and the poisons build up. Ends in a coma.

Yelena How long does this take?

Bulgakov A year. Maybe more.

Doctor Ha! . . . Sorry. And before you ask –

Bulgakov There's nothing can be done.

Doctor Nothing at all. Just to make it clear. I wouldn't want to engender false hope. False hope is not the business of a physician. Or a playwright, don't you think?

He stands.

Good day – Mrs Bulgakov. I am sorry.

Exit the Doctor.

Enter Anna, Grigory, Vasilly and Praskovya. They are emotional, upset. A flurry of comments and proposals.

Grigory Mikhail, we know.

Anna Yelena told us. It's terrible!

Grigory We think you should give up work. It's not important now.

Praskovya Exactly. If you don't want to work – don't let them force you. Not now.

Bulgakov tries in vain to calm them down.

Yelena I'm sorry, Misha, I had to talk to someone.

Bulgakov It's all right.

Anna And all of us – we think you should leave, with Yelena. If you want to. You should leave the Soviet Union. You've always wanted to travel. So go now.

The cupboard door slides open.

Sergei He can't leave without permission!

Vasilly Sergei – back in the cupboard!

He slides it shut.

Anna I have a cousin who lives just outside Leningrad. I will give you a letter. You can trust him. He will lead you across the ice, overnight, to Finland. From Helsinki, you can go anywhere.

Grigory Breathe free air, Mikhail.

Vasilly I have one or two trinkets you can sell, salvaged from the ruins.

Praskovya I know where you can get papers. And foreign currency.

Vasilly slides open the cupboard door.

Vasilly Sergei – you hear nothing of this!

He slides it shut again.

Yelena You see, Misha, we can go.

Bulgakov You're too kind, all of you. And you're right, all my life I have wanted to travel: to Paris, to Rome. But now – I don't want to go anywhere. I want to be with my friends and my colleagues, with the people I love. I want to stay here. I want to . . . I don't know – throw a party! Why not? To celebrate my good health! And if my illness were to turn up, uninvited, that's all right – we'll bring him in, we'll sit him down by the fire, put a drink in his hand then borrow a revolver and shoot the bastard!

Bulgakov takes Yelena's hand.
He addresses the others.

Now please. If you don't mind?

Vasilly Of course.

Exit Vasilly, Praskovya, Grigory and Anna.

Bulgakov Don't look at me like that, I'm not actually dead yet.

Yelena Please, Misha, don't talk like that. I don't –

Bulgakov – want to lose me! Less drama, more living, please. Honestly. It's not that bad. A change in status: that's all.

Yelena goes to sit on the bed, distressed.
  Bulgakov watches for a moment.
  Then he crosses to the gramophone.

Yelena Please, Misha, not just now.

Bulgakov Oh yes, now. Now more than ever.

He lifts a record and puts it on. He winds up the turntable and drops the stylus in place.
  The music could be a waltz or something contemporary, a piece of jazz, or something frivolous, like the cha-cha. But whatever, it is their tune.
  After a few bars, Bulgakov extends an arm.
  It has the air of a familiar ritual.

Madame.

He waits, arm outstretched.
  Eventually, Yelena smiles.
  She gets to her feet and crosses to him.
  She curtsies. He bows.
  They dance.
  During the dance, enter Vladimir and Stepan.
  They wait at the table.
  The dance finishes before the music.
  Bulgakov and Yelena kiss.
  She exits.

Bulgakov watches her go.
He lifts the stylus from the gramophone.
Removes the record.
He pulls on his coat.
He approaches the table.

Vladimir!

Vladimir Hello, Mikhail. Just wondered how you were getting on. Thought I could read whatever you've got so far.

Bulgakov I'm afraid there's nothing yet.

Vladimir So far, then: not so good.

Bulgakov It's difficult.

Vladimir For me – maybe. But you're a writer. You do this for a living.

Bulgakov It's difficult to get a real insight into the man.

Vladimir Read the books.

Bulgakov I read them!

Vladimir So read them some more! You have three weeks until his sixtieth birthday!

Bulgakov As an author, you have to love your characters.

Vladimir Of course. Even I can understand that. And I'm sure you will.

Bulgakov Really? You think so? You think I might find some empathy, some connection – with a loathsome psychopathic despot.

Vladimir smiles. Does not rise to the bait.

Vladimir Well, you did write to him, once, didn't you?

Bulgakov That . . . that was years ago.

31

Vladimir Eight years ago.

Vladimir produces a typed letter and reads.

'I can exist no longer, I am persecuted by authority . . . my work is banned from the stage . . . I have been brought to the verge of a nervous breakdown and request that you have me exiled from the USSR . . .' And then?

Bulgakov does not reply.

Perhaps you've forgotten. You wrote your whiney, self-pitying letter. And then one day, in your shitty little apartment, the telephone rings, and it rings, and eventually, you answer it. Do you remember?

Bulgakov Yes.

Vladimir Out of all the thousands of crackpots who write to him every day – he phoned you. And?

Bulgakov We had a conversation.

Vladimir You had a conversation. With him.

Vladimir produces a transcript. He reads the part of Stalin.

(*As Stalin.*) We received your letter. You want to go abroad? Perhaps we ought to let you. But tell me, have we really upset you so much?

Then the part of Bulgakov and so on.

(*As Bulgakov.*) Well . . . er . . . um . . . sir, you see, I must declare that I want to . . . I want to . . . to . . . Well, now I think about it, perhaps it would be best for me to remain here.

(*As Stalin.*) You are right. I think the same. Where would you like to work, Comrade? How about a job in the Moscow Art Theatre?

(*As Bulgakov.*) Yes, sir, I would like to work there. I did put in an application, but . . .

(*As Stalin.*) Put in another. Perhaps this time they will have a place for you.

Vladimir folds away the transcript.

And?

Bulgakov They did.

Vladimir He rescued your career.

Bulgakov Rescued it from his own oppression.

Vladimir Let's not split hairs. The point is: he gave you a second chance. *The White Guard* went on at the Art Theatre. Eight hundred performances later, you were the toast of literary Moscow. Now don't you owe him something?

Bulgakov says nothing.
Vladimir picks up the phone and dials.

Hello, Comrade, it's Vladimir. Listen – is anyone using the rooms at the moment? I've got a very important guest and I wanted to show him round.

He winks at Bulgakov.

Great. Now? OK? We'll be quick. I promise.

He hangs up.

Right. Let's go.

Vladimir leads Bulgakov across the stage.
Stepan follows.
They stop at the cupboard.
Vladimir draws it open.
The Cleaner, in an overall with a mop, steps out.
She also carries a folded tarpaulin which she hands to Stepan.

Stepan proceeds to unfold it on the floor.

Do you know what she does?

Bulgakov No.

Vladimir Guess.

Bulgakov No.

Vladimir Guess!

Bulgakov I have no idea.

Vladimir She cleans the tarpaulins.

Bulgakov still does not understand.

You see, down here, Bulgakov: this is where it actually happens. Before this, of course . . . the arrest . . . the interrogation . . . the confession . . . the trial . . . and then, you put on a white cotton shirt and you come down here. The wooden panelling prevents ricochets, which is also why we use a small-bore pistol –

Stepan draws out a pistol.

Like this one.

Vladimir pushes Bulgakov down on to his knees.
Stepan jabs the barrel into the top of Bulgakov's spine.

One shot to the back of the neck.

Stepan pulls the trigger. Click. Bulgakov jolts at the sound.

Often we need a second shot.

Stepan pulls the trigger again. Click.

You'd think that would be enough, right? You'd think two bullets, to the base of the brain – that would surely be enough to kill a man. But sometimes – we need a third.

And again. Click. Bulgakov jolts again.

And after that, she cleans the tarpaulin.

Stepan puts his gun away.
   Vladimir hauls the trembling Bulgakov back to his feet.
   Stepan folds up the tarp and hands it back to the Cleaner.
   She disappears back into the cupboard and Stepan slides the door closed.

Now I know you're a tough guy. You're not afraid of death – so I'm not going to threaten you. But I want to see some script by tomorrow morning. The opening scene. Whatever. I don't care. Words on the page. And don't think about yourself, Mikhail. Think about Yelena.

Enter Yelena in a nightgown. She gets into the bed and lies down.
   Vladimir and Stepan exit.
   For a beat, Bulgakov is alone.

Moonlight fades up on the bed.
   Yelena is asleep.
   Bulgakov crosses and sits on the bed. He is desperate, stuck.
   The telephone on its stand starts ringing.
   Yelena does not wake.
   The ringing continues.
   Bulgakov goes to the phone.
   He picks it up.

Bulgakov Hello?

The voice is male, rough.

Voice Can I help you, Comrade Bulgakov?

Bulgakov Who is this?

Voice Go to Mayakovskaya metro station. Take the northbound tunnel for three hundred metres. There you will find the entrance to a side tunnel which you should take, then climb the steps. Make sure you are not followed.

Bulgakov Who are you?

Voice I'll be waiting.

> *Click. The line goes dead.*
> *Bulgakov replaces the receiver.*
> *A pause.*
> *Then he goes to the bed and grabs his coat.*
> *He goes to the front of the stage.*
> *Yelena wakes.*
> *She pulls on a gown.*

Yelena Mikhail! Mikhail!

> *She cannot find him.*
> *She exits, calling:*

Vasilly! Praskovya!

> *Bulgakov crosses to the desk.*
> *He stops and turns to face the cupboard.*
> *The door slides open.*
> *Slowly, a man emerges, silhouetted from behind.*
> *Bulgakov steps back in shock.*
> *The light changes to reveal his face.*

Stalin So who did you expect?

> *Bulgakov is speechless.*
> *The dictator is in his favoured peasant garb: boots, baggy tunic, simple jacket buttoned up.*
> *He holds an unlit pipe which he sucks on from time to time.*

You know where you are?

He smiles, continues with theatrical mock secrecy.

Directly beneath the Kremlin!

Bulgakov is still bewildered.

When they were building the metro – it was my idea – secret tunnel, snug little cubbyhole for yours truly – I always knew it would come in useful some day – and look – here we are! Just you and me! Now why don't you sit down?

Bulgakov slumps on to a chair.

Vodka?

He pours two. Passes one to Bulgakov, who drinks. Stalin holds his but does not drink.

I hear you're struggling.

A beat.

With the play, Mikhail. It's supposed to be a surprise. But I hate surprises. More than anything in the world, I think, I hate surprises. It's supposed to be kept a secret – a secret – from me! – which, frankly, is annoying – but some other time . . . Anyway: you're struggling.

Bulgakov Yes, yes, I am . . . sir.

Stalin Please. Joseph.

Bulgakov Yes, Joseph, sir, I mean, no, it's not going well.

Stalin Not going at all, as I understand it.

Bulgakov You're right.

Stalin I think we need candour from the start. The good news is that I can help you. In fact I want to help you. It would be a privilege for me, a mere philistine, to collaborate with the great Mikhail Bulgakov. To collaborate! I mean, just to watch you create, that would be the privilege. You see, I love the theatre. I always have. You know, the Art Theatre, they gave me this badge. Look, a little . . .

Bulgakov Seagull.

Stalin Yes, a seagull. In recognition of my support. You know when they pinned it on, I was in tears. I felt the hand of . . . of . . .

Overcome with emotion, he cannot finish.

Bulgakov Chekhov?

Stalin Yes – upon my shoulder! And yet I knew I was unworthy. You know what they call me – The Great Friend of Actors and Theatre, with a capital letter at the start of each word, as though that makes it true. Still, I love the theatre. And I love your work. *The White Guard* – fifteen times! I am probably your number-one fan. Almost to the point of obsession. Scary! OK, so you're quite clearly an enemy of the state.

Bulgakov attempts to disagree.

No, no – let's call a spade a spade. It's what you are. A class enemy. A talented class enemy, it must be said, but that only makes you more dangerous. You are a subversive worm burrowing its way into the body of the nation intent upon devouring us from within. Nevertheless, allowing for that: I like you. So what's up?

Bulgakov Well . . .

Stalin Joseph.

Bulgakov Joseph, it's like this. I've read a lot about you, but I don't think I'm getting –

Stalin The real me.

Bulgakov The real you.

Stalin Tricky. But not any more. Now you can get it from the horse's mouth – though don't ever, ever refer to me that way in public. I have ideas. A couple of scenes.

Bulgakov Scenes?

Stalin Yes. Characters, dialogue, action. If that's all right with you?

Bulgakov Yes. Sir. Joseph. Of course.

Stalin Now, the clock is ticking. Shall we begin?

He claps Bulgakov on the shoulder and ushers him to the desk. He feeds a sheet of paper.

Act One, Scene One – hold on – I forgot – you have a title?

Bulgakov *Young Joseph.*

Stalin *Young Joseph.* I like it! It's about me when I was young. It's better than your others, if you don't mind me saying so. Less pretentious. I like a title that tells it like it is. Ivan the Terrible. Peter the Great. Young Joseph the . . . whatever. 'Heroic' would fit, obviously, but I leave it up to you. Whatever you choose. Doesn't have to be 'Heroic'. Could be another word altogether meaning heroic. What do you think?

Bulgakov I was just going to call it *Young Joseph.*

Stalin Just . . . *Young Joseph.* Nothing else? That's all?

A silence as Stalin absorbs.

Bulgakov I could change it –

Stalin No! You're the playwright. It's your play. If you say it's *Young Joseph the* . . . nothing, then that's what it is. I'll just have to learn to live with it. *Young . . . Joseph . . .*

Bulgakov I'm sorry.

Stalin Don't apologise. It's your play. Now where were we? Act One, Scene One – the Russian orthodox seminary in Tbilisi.

Bulgakov types as Stalin dictates too fast.

Young Joseph is learning to be a priest. This cobbler's son, born into poverty, his nature forged on the rough tough streets of Gori, his father driven to despair and drink by capitalist exploitation – this boy has clawed his way up through intelligence and endeavour – What's wrong?

Bulgakov Could you slow down?

Stalin studies him.

Stalin Are you ill?

Bulgakov No.

Stalin You don't look so well. Maybe it's just this light . . . your skin, it's sort of . . .

Bulgakov I'm fine. Just nerves. That's all.

Stalin Of course. The artistic temperament. I should have allowed for that. Anyway – what have I got you sitting there for? You're not the typist, you're the genius! Let's swap! You come and sit here – leave the slave labour to me.

Bulgakov What?

Stalin helps him out of the chair and sits down himself.
He rolls up his sleeves. Smooths his hair.
Sucks on his pipe.

Stalin There, that's better. Now: here we go . . .

And he's off. A real speed typist.
Bulgakov sits and watches.

*Stalin continues typing, lost in thought, his lips
moving silently as he types. The roller of the machine
is fairly zinging back and forth.*
Bulgakov drinks his vodka. He sits back.
Closes his eyes.
Stalin finishes.
*He puts the typed sheets inside a large envelope and
leaves this on the table beside Bulgakov.*
*Stalin opens the cupboard and disappears inside,
pulling the door closed.*
Bulgakov awakes. Disoriented at first.
He jumps up. Looks around. He is alone.
Checks his watch.
He sees the envelope.
He picks it up and looks inside.
He looks around. Goes to front of stage.
Flustered in the daylight.

*Enter Yelena, Vasilly, Praskovya and Sergei around
the table.*

Vasilly You mustn't worry, my dear. He'll be home soon.

Praskovya More likely you will never see him again.

Sergei I will go out and search, Comrade Madame
Bulgakov.

Yelena That's very kind of you, Sergei.

Sergei And if he does not return, I will look after you
for the rest of your life, like a son.

Yelena That's also very kind, in its own way.

Bulgakov approaches, still holding the envelope.

Misha!

Bulgakov What's wrong?

Yelena Where have you been?

He hugs her.

Bulgakov I went for a walk – to work.

Yelena At night? At the Lubyanka?

Bulgakov I couldn't sleep – Yelena, I think I've found a way –

Yelena You could have left a note. I was worried.

Bulgakov There's nothing to worry about. A way to do it – to write what they want. They can have this, and I'll have my work. I think it's all going to be all right!

A harsh knock.
Enter Vladimir and Stepan.

Vladimir Bulgakov!

Bulgakov spins round, holding out the envelope.

Bulgakov For you.

Vladimir takes it, a little put out at being trumped.

Vladimir All right, everyone out except the artist.

Exit Vasilly, Praskovya and Sergei (into cupboard).
Yelena remains.

Madame Bulgakov, good morning to you.

Yelena Sergei!

Sergei Comrade Madame Bulgakov?

She kisses Bulgakov on the cheek and steps into the cupboard.
She pulls it closed.

Vladimir I tell you, that's not right.

Bulgakov Are you going to read it or not?

Vladimir takes the pages out of the envelope.

He reads to himself.

I hope it meets with your approval.

Vladimir It's . . . it's good. It's very good. I never doubted you. I knew you could do it. I love the way you capture the essence of the boy. His intelligence, his bravery – even as a child. It's moving. When Stalin sees this – I'll probably get a promotion.

Bulgakov I'm very happy for you.

Vladimir You keep writing. I'll start casting.

Bulgakov Casting? All we have is one scene –

Vladimir Mikhail, we have a deadline. There is so much to do! Sets, costumes, rehearsals –

Bulgakov Yes, but, normally, there's a director involved.

Vladimir There is a director involved.

He opens his arms wide.
Bulgakov says nothing.

You don't think I'm qualified? Go on, say it. Be as hurtful as you like.

Bulgakov You're a secret policeman.

Vladimir Is that all I am to you? That's how you think of me? Am I not allowed other qualities? Literary sensitivity, imagination, a willingness to explore ideas through sound and light, voice and motion? Stepan – do I not have literary sensitivity?

Stepan says nothing. His expression does not change.

You see? So it's decided then. Genius, Bulgakov.

Bulgakov You're too kind.

Vladimir No. I mean I'm a genius. For hiring you.

Vladimir exits, followed by Stepan.
Enter Stalin.
He sits at the table, feeds in a sheet and starts typing.
Bulgakov pulls on his coat.
He crosses to the desk where Stalin is still typing.
Stalin does not acknowledge Bulgakov until he has finished a passage and returned the roller.

Stalin You're late.

Bulgakov I'm sorry.

Stalin Actually, I was early. Truth is, I wanted to be early, I wanted to get started. All day, I've been so excited. Couldn't think about anything else. So much more enjoyable than all that yackety-yak at the Politburo and Central Committee and God knows what else! When I was young, you know, I wrote poetry.

Bulgakov Really?

Stalin Yes. We Georgians, we're all poets.

Bulgakov I'd love to read it some day.

Stalin If I thought for one moment that you really meant that – I'd make you read it! But my guess is you'd sooner be tortured in the Lubyanka. I know I would!

Bulgakov forces a smile.

Isn't it wonderful to be creative?

Bulgakov It is. Yes. To make something –

Stalin – from nothing.

He pours two glasses of vodka. They toast.

To creativity.

Stalin slams down his glass and spools out the sheet of paper. Adds it to a few pages of manuscript.

So here's where I am. I've written another scene in the seminary. Young Joseph is the outsider – poor kid, wrong side of the tracks – who becomes the leader of the rebellion against the oppressive brutality of the priests.

Bulgakov So you want to prefigure the events of the revolution.

Stalin Exactly.

Bulgakov To illustrate your – young Joseph's – precocity. His talent for organising.

Stalin And inspiring.

Bulgakov Of course. And inspiring.

Enter two Actors with a sack of props and costumes.

Stalin Those bastards! They educated me, but they couldn't break me!

He hands the manuscript to Bulgakov.

Actor One You bastards! You can educate me but you can never break me!

Exit Bulgakov and Stalin.
Enter Vladimir and Stepan.
Vladimir pulls up a chair and watches the actors.
Stepan lurks behind him, impassive.

Actor Two You dog! How dare you speak to me like that! You think we'll let you get away with free thought! We'll beat it out of you, I swear to God we will!

Actor One Never!

Actor Two beats Actor One.

Actor Two There! Now spend some time in the punishment cell, you upstart proletarian! Son of cobbler!

Actor One stands and pulls on a cassock.

45

Actor One This young Dzughashvili – he's a tough one.

Actor Two Too tough. He combines righteous fury with piercing intellect.

Actor One I've never met anything like him.

Actor Two He's been reading Marx and converting his fellow students.

Actor One We'll give him one more chance. If he won't give in . . .

Actor Two I understand.

Actor One takes off the cassock.

All right, Joseph, this is your last chance. Renounce Marx, conform to our rules and pledge loyalty to the Tsar.

Actor One Never. I cannot ignore the needs of the people. My path has been chosen. It is not an easy one but it is the right one.

Actor Two Get out of here! You are expelled!

Enter Bulgakov. He watches.

Actor One Don't worry. I'm leaving. And I promise – I'll never look back.

Exit Actors One and Two.

Vladimir Bulgakov! Did you catch it?

Bulgakov Just the end.

Vladimir It's fantastic, Mikhail.

Bulgakov You don't think it's a little too obviously . . .

Vladimir What?

Bulgakov Uncritical. I wouldn't want to overdo it.

Vladimir You nailed the guy, Mikhail, you captured him. Every inflection feels so authentic. It's a work of art.

Bulgakov I must admit, I do feel I've made contact with the character.

Vladimir So what was it? I'm curious. What unlocked it for you?

Bulgakov It just started to fall into place, really.

Vladimir Our little chat in the cellars, perhaps?

Bulgakov Perhaps.

Vladimir I wouldn't like to think it was just that. I mean, I want you and I to have a rich and fruitful creative relationship and I appreciate that in my role as producer/director, I may have overstepped the mark in threatening to shoot your wife.

Bulgakov Don't worry.

Vladimir I feel bad about it.

Bulgakov It's your working method.

Vladimir Exactly. That's all. And for the record, in truth, I would never have shot Yelena.

Bulgakov You wouldn't?

Vladimir No. A mock execution, perhaps.

Bulgakov Yes.

Vladimir A whole series of bewildering, traumatic mock executions designed to leave her emotionally fractured and psychologically disabled. But never the live round.

Bulgakov That's all the difference.

Vladimir Isn't it just!

Bulgakov You're going soft.

Vladimir I wouldn't jeopardise the project.

A beat.
Bulgakov hands over the latest pages.

Now come on – I'll buy you breakfast.

Exit Vladimir with Bulgakov.
Stepan stands for a beat.
Then he follows as Praskovya enters.
She sits at the table.
Enter Vasilly in a bathrobe. Hair still wet. Full of joy.

Vasilly Look at this! Look at me! Fresh from a bath! Hot running water! Gallons of the stuff!

Praskovya It won't last.

Vasilly I left the tap running just to check – if anything it was getting hotter. Practically a jet of steam –

Praskovya Must be a mistake.

Vasilly Providence, Praskovya! Justice!

He slides open the cupboard door and bellows in to a sleeping Sergei.

Long live the Revolution!

Sergei wakes. Tumbles out and to his feet.

Sergei Is it time for work?

Vasilly It is time for a bath, you unwashed proletarian!

He spins round.

And is it my imagination or is that . . .

Praskovya It's coffee.

Vasilly Yes!

Enter Bulgakov, carrying a large bunch of roses.
Enter Yelena from the other direction.

Yelena Misha!

Bulgakov My darling. For you.

She takes them.

Yelena But where from?

Bulgakov There was a woman selling them – just around the corner.

Yelena But no one sells roses in Moscow in December!

Bulgakov Smell them and tell me if they're not real.

They cross towards the bed.

Vasilly Sergei! To the bath, Comrade!

He exits, pulling Sergei with him.

Praskovya I'll get the soap.

She exits.

Yelena You shouldn't.

Bulgakov I should.

She kisses him.

Yelena You look better, Misha.

Bulgakov I feel no worse.

Yelena Perhaps it's not . . .

Bulgakov I'm not thinking about it. Let's not talk about it. Remember, I'm alive, you're alive, and so on.

He holds her hand.
They dance a few steps, making the music of their favourite tune.

They kiss.
They sit, then recline, on the bed.
The lights fade to moonlight.

Bulgakov sits up.
He stands and pulls on his coat.
He goes to the front stage.
Exit Yelena.
Bulgakov crosses to the desk.
No sign of Stalin.
Suddenly the cupboard door slides opens and closes very quickly.
Stalin steps forward.
He is clutching a thick pile of files and notes –
administrative paperwork.

Stalin I'm late – I know.

Bulgakov It's all right.

Stalin I have other things to do, you know.

Bulgakov Of course. I didn't say anything.

Stalin A country to run.

Bulgakov Yes, I know. I'm sorry.

Stalin dumps the paperwork on the desk and sits down at the typewriter.

Stalin Never stops, you know. Always something.

Bulgakov It's a big responsibility.

Stalin Does anyone think so?

Bulgakov The people are grateful.

Stalin Are they? I'll take your word on that. Now where was I?

He settles himself in at the desk.

Bulgakov The seminary. You were expelled.

Stalin Yes! Now – here's what I was thinking. We jump forward one year. The oil town of Batumi. I am now a fully active, full-time Bolshevik revolutionary. Fast becoming the Lenin of south-west Georgia! – Strike the 'south-west'!

Bulgakov It's good. You're keeping it moving.

Stalin Exactly! That's what I thought. There's a dynamism in my life –

Bulgakov Reflected in the text.

Stalin You and me, Mikhail – two minds with as but one thought.

Bulgakov So what happens in Batumi?

Stalin I've infiltrated the Rothschild oil refinery, spreading the credo of armed insurrection among the workers. On a personal level, I'm living in an apartment. There's a girl there.

Bulgakov Good.

Stalin And guess what?

Bulgakov She's in love with you.

Stalin It's true. And believe me, she wasn't the only one.

Bulgakov Romance. Always popular.

Stalin OK. Here goes.

He feeds in the paper.

One moment – if I'm doing your job, why don't you do mine?

Bulgakov Do yours?

Stalin Yeah. See those papers – that's a summary of the steel output for the entire USSR, broken down into individual republics, regions, provinces, mills, foundries, shifts. What you have to do –

Bulgakov Me!

Stalin – is make a note beside each one, more or less. 'Increased output required!' 'Must work harder!' 'More steel needed – increase by 59 per cent in six months!' Stuff like that.

Bulgakov I can't do that.

Stalin Of course you can. Go on, Mikhail. Make a note.

He thrusts one of the sheets towards Bulgakov.

Go on. Just try it. Just once . . .

Bulgakov picks up a pen. Hesitates. Then writes in the margin.
Stalin reads over his shoulder.

Stalin 'More steel or else!' Oh boy! When you get angry, you really get angry! '. . . or else!' – might use that one myself someday. OK. Now sign. J.S.

Bulgakov J.S.?

Stalin That's me.

Bulgakov Yes – I know, but . . .

Stalin What's the problem?

Bulgakov I can't sign your initials. That's illegal!

Stalin You've done the hard bit, the creative work, but unless you sign it, it isn't going to work. J . . . S . . . J.S., J for Joseph –

Bulgakov I can't!

Stalin Go on, Mikhail. Sign it. It's our little secret. No one will ever know.

Bulgakov No one?

Stalin No one.

> *Suddenly, with a flourish, Bulgakov signs the order and throws down the pen.*
> *They begin giggling.*
> *Stalin punches Bulgakov affectionately on the shoulder.*
> *Bulgakov punches him back, even harder.*
> *They both giggle even more at Bulgakov's audacity.*
> *Enter the two Actors, followed by Vladimir and Stepan.*
> *Bulgakov and Stalin exit, giggling like naughty boys.*
> *Actor Two pulls on a dress.*

Actor One Good news, Kato, I have secured employment at the Rothschild oil refinery. From within, I can convert workers to Marxism and recruit them to the cause. It's only a matter of time before we bring the whole edifice of capitalist imperialism crashing to its knees!

Actor Two Oh Joseph, it's incredible. Only you could have achieved so much so soon.

Actor One It's nothing.

Actor Two You must be busy.

Actor One Of course.

Actor Two And is there time for anything else in your life?

Actor One My spare time is devoted to my passion.

Actor Two Your passion?

Actor One Reading. Marx mainly. And Lenin, of course.

Actor Two Is that all?

Actor One Oh no. I also write propaganda.

Actor Two OK. Right. And anything else?

Actor One Fund-raising.

Actor Two No! I mean anything else that doesn't relate to fomenting the overthrow of the Romanov dynasty?

Actor One Sorry?

Actor Two takes the hand of Actor One.

Actor Two Love, Joseph. Is there time in your life for love?

Actor One It will lead only to heartbreak, my dear. For mine is a restless soul. It cannot be tamed, nor held. I am here today and gone tomorrow.

Actor Two Oh, Joseph, I don't care – then I shall love you today and damn tomorrow!

They kiss.
Enter Grigory carrying a cup.

Vladimir Good kissing. Break for lunch, back in one hour.

Exit Vladimir, Stepan, the two Actors.
Grigory sits at the table and waits.
Enter Bulgakov.

Bulgakov Grigory!

Grigory Hello, Mikhail. Vasilly let me in.

Bulgakov That's fine. Always good to see you.

Grigory He said I should help myself to some coffee too. It's very good.

Bulgakov You're welcome. Surprised he didn't tell you to have a bath.

Grigory He did. And the heating too . . .

Bulgakov Yes. It's an improvement.

Grigory So how's it going?

Bulgakov It's a hack job. Mindless. But I'm getting through it.

Grigory Is that all?

Bulgakov How else could it be?

Grigory I hear it's going well. Yelena told Anna. Anna told me. That you're making progress. And that you're thriving. Rejuvenated, they said. Mentally and physically.

Bulgakov That's perhaps going a little too far.

Grigory You certainly look better. Never liked to say before, but there was a tinge – in your skin –

Bulgakov It's the nephrosclerosis – the pigmentation –

Grigory Really? Because in this light, I can . . . I can hardly see it at all, really.

Bulgakov You must tell me: your work, your situation – how's it going?

Grigory I'd like to, if you don't mind – I mean that's partly why I'm here. My situation.

A knock at the door.

Bulgakov One moment.

Enter the Driver.

Driver Mr Bulgakov?

Bulgakov Yes?

Driver Your car is ready.

Bulgakov My car?

Grigory Your car?

Driver Yes, sir. Your car is ready.

Bulgakov My car? Who arranged that?

Driver I just take orders, sir.

Bulgakov Am I being arrested?

Driver I'm not a policeman, sir. I'm just a driver.

Bulgakov Then where are you taking me?

Driver To work. And then home again. And anywhere else you want to go.

Bulgakov Anywhere else I want to go?

Grigory Tell him you want to go to Paris.

Driver I'll wait outside, sir.

The Driver exits.

Bulgakov Grigory – please understand – this is something of a surprise to me –

Grigory Nice surprise. Coffee, heating, car – where's it going to end?

Bulgakov Anyway, tell me: what's happening?

Grigory You have to go, Mikhail – your car is waiting.

Bulgakov No, forget that – I want to know. Your situation – what's happened.

Grigory It's all right. Some other time. Honestly.

Bulgakov You're sure?

Grigory Yes.

Bulgakov It's just . . .

Grigory I know. Don't worry about it. You're busy. It's good.

Bulgakov Call round again. Promise?

Grigory Yes!

Bulgakov Let's meet. Coffee. Dinner. You can tell me all. I'll look forward to it.

Grigory You'd better go.

> *A shake of the hands.*
> *Bulgakov exits.*
> *Grigory is left alone.*
> *He sips his coffee.*
> *A beat.*
> *He tips the rest away.*

> *Exit Grigory as the two Actors enter.*
> *They are mock-fighting, One in greatcoat and Stalin moustache, Two in a cossack's hat with sword and hobby horse.*
> *Vladimir follows closely, directing.*
> *Stepan enters and watches.*
> *Bulgakov enters and sits down.*

Vladimir You cut them down with your swords! You pitiless Cossack bastards! Young Joseph – you stand your ground – yield to no man – you witness the senseless slaughter of your comrades but 'with no thought of self-preservation, he throws himself forward to tend the wounded'. OK, when you're ready.

> *He walks back and sits near Bulgakov.*
> *They watch the Actors finding their way through the scene.*

Nice suit.

Bulgakov Thanks.

> *A beat.*

Someone arranged a car for me.

> *Eventually Vladimir responds.*

Vladimir A car?

Bulgakov With a driver.

Vladimir Lucky you.

Bulgakov What's wrong?

Vladimir Nothing.

Bulgakov Then why 'lucky you'?

Vladimir I just mean you're lucky, that's all! Why does everything have to mean something? You've got a car. End of story.

Bulgakov And a driver.

Vladimir And a driver. Big fucking deal.

A pause.

Bulgakov Do you like the scene? Are you happy with how it's going? I mean, I must admit, I was sceptical. You know I was, about the whole project. I couldn't see it. But now – I think it's starting to take shape. I actually think it could even be quite . . . you know . . .

Vladimir I used to have one.

Bulgakov What?

Vladimir A car. And a driver. But they took it away. Just a couple of days ago, as it happens. 'Reallocation of resources'.

Bulgakov Oh. Vladimir – I'm sorry.

Vladimir Not your fault.

Bulgakov No.

Vladimir I didn't say it was your fault. In fact I'm sure it's a coincidence. I'm sure the two events of your being given a car and mine being taken away – at exactly the same time – are not in any way whatsoever connected.

A beat.

Unless you want to tell me otherwise?

On the platform. Actor Two rehearses his sabre-swooshing charge.

Actor One Oh God, I've been cut! Help! Help!

He is bleeding. He bursts into tears.
Vladimir jumps out of his seat.

Vladimir All right! Stop there! Someone get a bandage – young Joseph's been wounded!

Exit Vladimir and Stepan and two Actors.
Enter Stalin with a bundle of paperwork.
He sits at the desk. Begins typing. Lost in his own thoughts and story.
Bulgakov also sits. He works his way through the paperwork.
Bulgakov pauses.

Bulgakov Thank you.

Stalin doesn't stop.

Stalin For what?

Bulgakov The car.

Stalin Nothing to do with me.

He continues to type.

Bulgakov And the hot water.

Stalin I'll be honest with you, Mikhail – I don't personally heat the water of every citizen in the Union. I don't slope off from the Central Committee of an evening to stack your boiler with coal. But if you do have hot water, I might come round for a bath. The plumbing in the Kremlin is not for the faint-hearted.

Stalin continues typing.
Bulgakov watches for a moment. Then returns to
the documents.

Bulgakov Hey! Look at this!

Stalin What is it?

Bulgakov Steel output in Belarus – 'Increasing 5 per cent per day'! 'Will double in less than a month'!

Stalin Isn't that amazing?

Bulgakov Yes. But it's not . . . I mean, it's not true, is it?

Stalin Isn't it? Why not?

Bulgakov You mean . . .

Stalin Why should something not be true, Mikhail?

Bulgakov But it's . . . it's exactly what I asked for.

Stalin Cause and effect.

Bulgakov All I had to do was write it. And that made it happen. I made it happen. I made steel output increase, just by . . .

Stalin Bulgakov: you're a natural.

Stalin returns to typing.
Bulgakov returns to the documents.
A few moments pass, each man hard at work.
Then Bulgakov's face clouds.

Bulgakov Hold on. This is more difficult.

Stalin What's up?

Bulgakov The cities need grain. To feed the industrial workers.

Stalin Can't argue with that.

Bulgakov But the farmers – the peasants – well, it seems that they're holding on to the supply – refusing to sell it.

Stalin Really? Why would they do that?

Bulgakov reads from the reports.

Bulgakov Well – they claim the harvest is poor and that they need to feed themselves and their families and that they need to keep some grain to plant for next year's harvest otherwise it'll be even worse!

Stalin resumes his typing. Bulgakov follows his own stream of consciousness.

So it's a question of judging whose needs are greater. Also trying to balance a quick fix against the possibility of longer-term problems –

Stalin Mikhail – I know I asked, but actually – I'm not interested.

Bulgakov It seems the only way to get the grain would be to send in troops to take it, at gunpoint if necessary. But that doesn't seem right.

Stalin ignores him.

What do you think?

Stalin I'm doing your job. I'm working on my play. Your play. Do mine. Please.

Bulgakov I'm not qualified!

Stalin Neither was I! Once upon a time. So what I did was, I worked it out as I was going along. Like I'm not qualified to write a play – but I'm doing the best I can. That's all anyone can ask of you. This is what it's like when you govern. You sit here, in an office in Moscow. And out there, there's a hundred million peasants who cannot read. They hate you. They don't trust you. But you have a country to run. Targets to fulfil. An industrial base to secure, to expand. You have cities waiting to be fed. No one says it's easy! But someone has to do it. Someone has to be in charge. Who's it going to be? A forward-looking progressive regime swept to power on a popular revolution, or a bunch of unelected self-interested farmers?

Bulgakov What about next year's harvest?

Stalin What about next week's bread?

Bulgakov What shall I do?

Stalin Make a decision, Mikhail. And sign it J.S.

He continues. Discussion closed.
He concludes typing. Pulls out the sheets, folds them and holds them out for Bulgakov.
Bulgakov hesitates for a moment, then scrawls on the documents.
Bulgakov takes the manuscript from Stalin.
Exit Stalin.

Enter Yelena.
Bulgakov crosses to meet her.

Bulgakov I'm sure this is a mistake.

Yelena There's no mistake.

She produces a telegram from her handbag.

'M. Bulgakov to attend Lenin Clinic this day 09.00 for examination.' That's what it says.

Bulgakov The Lenin Clinic is only for the elite. The privileged few.

Yelena That's not true. All facilities are equally open to all citizens. The fact that you've been sent an appointment is proof in itself.

He looks at her.

I'm joking. Be thankful.

Bulgakov For what?

Yelena Perhaps they have a new treatment.

Bulgakov There is no treatment.

He sits at the table. Yelena stands behind.
Enter the Doctor.
The Doctor is now immaculately turned out.
A pretty, pristine Nurse is in attendance.

Doctor Mr and Mrs Bulgakov! What a delight, what an honour to make your aquaintance! Please, please, sit down! Did you meet my assistant, my little Ninotchka? She used to be an actress, until I rescued her from that delinquent profession. Coffee? Vodka? Whatever you like? Now, let's have a look.

He opens a folder.

So, Mikhail: your blood pressure is now normal. That's good, isn't it? Really good. And new analysis of both the blood and the urine is . . . also . . . one hundred per cent normal. So, today, we have literally no evidence of disease. *C'est le malade imaginaire.*

Bulgakov That's impossible.

Doctor How do you feel?

Bulgakov I feel well.

Doctor As you should. Because there is nothing wrong with you, or at least nothing that a bit of red meat and fresh fruit wouldn't help.

Bulgakov But there is no treatment for nephrosclerosis! It is a progressive condition leading to failure of the kidneys.

63

Doctor Pardon me, sir, but I am a doctor too – indeed, I am a specialist in this very field, and I do know about nephrosclerosis.

Bulgakov It does not simply disappear!

Doctor Except in your case, it would appear that it has. A miracle! Or more prosaically, the original diagnosis was wrong.

Bulgakov I don't think so. The blood tests were unequivocal.

Doctor That leaves the miracle. Anyway, all you need, sir, is building up. Some meat on your ribs, some iron in your bloodstream.

He lifts out a printed pad, writes on it, then completes the job with a big stamp.

Take this. Your driver will know where to go.

Bulgakov How did you know I have a driver?

Doctor Good day, Mr Bulgakov. Your life is saved!

Yelena Doctor –

Doctor Madame – thank you, and farewell.

He kisses her hand.
    Doctor and Nurse exit.
    Music begins.
    Doctor and Nurse return, now dressed as a butler and maid.
    They each draw a trolley laden with fruit, meat, delicacies, wine, etc.
    Bulgakov and Yelena watch, astonished, as the table is set for a sumptuous feast.
    All choreographed to the music.

Vasilly, Praskovya, Sergei enter to assist with the setting, the men bringing more chairs. All three are dressed up in previously unseen finery.

With a final flourish of music and dance, Doctor and Nurse depart.

A beat.

Vasilly lifts a banana. Peels it. Takes a bite.

Vasilly Nice work, Bulgakov.

End of Act One.

Act Two

The set is as before.

Grigory, Anna, Vasilly, Praskovya and Sergei are all gathered round the table, dressed up for the big dinner, sipping champagne.

Yelena helps Bulgakov with his bow tie near the bed.

Enter Vladimir and his wife Eva, also dressed up for dinner.

They cross the stage, followed by Stepan, who is dressed the same as usual.

Vladimir Relax!

Eva I am.

Vladimir Just because he's show-business – it doesn't mean he's better than us. Socially, I mean. We're not punching above our weight here. I am a respected representative of the organ of state security and you are my wife. We are not intimidated by fancy-pants intellectuals.

Eva I know that.

Vladimir We can hold our own.

Eva Yes.

Vladimir You play the piano. I was in the school show at the age of ten. We're not strangers to his world.

Eva I know that, dear.

Vladimir Just try not to be too gushing.

Bulgakov Vladimir! Please, come on in.

Vladimir So kind of you to invite us! We never expected – I mean it's not like we gave you the job just so we could, you know, come round socially and . . . Gosh! Is it hot in here?

Bulgakov takes coats from Vladimir and Eva.
Stepan keeps his on throughout.

Yelena Well, I've been hearing so much about you.

Eva The same here.

Vladimir Nice place, Bulgakov. Warm too. All right for some.

Bulgakov In paradise, Vladimir, everyone is equal –

Vladimir But in Moscow . . .

They all laugh. Apart from Stepan.

Bulgakov Come on in. Sit down. Set to!

They sit. They eat. They chatter.
Then Grigory is talking to Vladimir.

Grigory So they want me to write a self-criticism. They say if I don't, then all my work will be banned. And if I do, it'll probably be banned anyway.

Vladimir That is such nonsense. I'm sorry to hear it – young guy like you.

Grigory Yeah, so I'm going to write one. I'm going to admit to my failings: too talented, too handsome, too successful.

They laugh.

Vladimir If there's anything I can do . . .

Grigory They don't scare me.

Vasilly You know, I had news from the old estate the other day. What do you think of this? Troops came to collect the grain. But the harvest has been poor. There isn't enough to meet the targets that have been set. The peasants were willing to hand over their surplus, but they need to keep some for themselves and their families. But the soldiers wanted all of it. There was a struggle. Gunshots. Some men were killed. The grain was taken. So now they starve.

Yelena That's terrible.

Vasilly Yes. And what I hear is that there have been instances of men, women and children eating other men, women and children.

Sergei That's not true.

Vasilly Isn't it?

Sergei No. We're not savages. This is the twentieth century. Those things don't happen here.

Vasilly Well that's all right, then.

Bulgakov Vasilly – it may or may not be true, but surely you'd have to accept that . . .

Vasilly What?

Bulgakov Well . . . that it's not easy. To govern, I mean. It's tough, it must be. Very hard, to make decisions.

Vasilly Is it?

Bulgakov You sit in an office in Moscow. There's a hundred million peasants who can't read. Cities waiting to be fed. And you ask yourself – who's in charge here?

Vasilly What's that got to do with it? I was talking about cannibalism.

Bulgakov Yes, but who's to say – what it's to be: next year's harvest or next week's bread? I'm saying it's not easy.

Vasilly Perhaps I was wrong. Perhaps 'who's in charge' is actually what it's all about. I can understand it now, from that perspective. Death by starvation: it's the only language they understand.

Bulgakov I can't believe that was the purpose of the decision.

Vasilly And what makes you so sure?

Silence.
Yelena stands up.

Yelena Would anyone like to dance?

She hurries up to the gramophone and starts it up.
Lights fade.
Soon all are up dancing to American jazz.
Stepan crudely and blatantly gropes Eva.
She firmly but politely pushes him away.
He returns to grope her again.
Bulgakov ushers Grigory away.
As they walk away, there is a short scuffle as
Vladimir separates Stepan from Eva.
Bulgakov and Grigory move to front of stage.
Lights down behind them and the jazz fades.
The table is cleared by the guests and by the Doctor
and Nurse (as butler and maid).
Exit all except the two men.
Bulgakov produces cigars. They light up.

Bulgakov I'm sorry. I didn't know they had demanded a self-criticism.

Grigory I'm worried.

Bulgakov Grigory, you are a great novelist. Those talentless dimwits at the Writers' Union – I tell you, it's not politics, it's envy. Stand your ground.

Grigory It's not me I'm worried about.

Bulgakov My health is good.

Grigory Not your health either. This play you're writing.

Bulgakov What about it?

Grigory You were always the guy we looked up to. When they collected signatures to denounce someone, you stood your ground, never put your name to one. You always battled against the censor, found a way through if there was one, and if not – then try again! But this . . . You had to do it, right?

Bulgakov Yes.

Grigory No choice?

Bulgakov No.

Grigory They would have arrested Yelena?

Bulgakov Yes.

Grigory Well then, I understand –

Bulgakov But maybe it's good for me.

Grigory Oh, it's certainly that.

Bulgakov Not materially. I mean, as a writer. Sometimes it's good to look at things from a different point of view.

Grigory I think I preferred your point of view.

Bulgakov I struggled for years, Grigory.

Grigory That's right. We all know that, Mikhail. We watched you struggle. And we admired that. I have worshipped and been inspired by your perseverance. It defines you. Or at least it did.

Bulgakov I haven't given in. I'm still the same. I'm just – why do I have to apologise?

Grigory They say that when a man is going to drown, when he finally gives up the struggle – it's sort of blissful, for a moment. And then he drowns.

Bulgakov stubs out his cigar.

Bulgakov Are you finished?

A beat.
Grigory drops his cigar and grinds it with his heel.
He exits.
Bulgakov stands for a beat.
He turns and crosses to the bed.
Enter Yelena.
She sits, facing away, brushing her hair, preparing for bed.
Yelena is silent.

What's wrong?

Yelena Nothing.

Bulgakov Do you think I've done something wrong?

Yelena No. Why do you ask that?

Bulgakov Everyone had a good time, didn't they?

She says nothing.

I mean, Vasilly's story. That's nothing to do with me.

Yelena Who said it was?

Bulgakov It's probably not even true. He talks such . . .
You know.

Yelena Yes. I know.

A pause.

Can I read it?

Bulgakov Yes, of course.

A pause.

Only not yet, if that's all right. I'd like your opinion,
I really would.

Yelena But not yet.

They sit in silence for a moment.
Yelena exits.
Bulgakov pulls his coat on.

Enter Stalin. He takes his seat at the table and places a bundle of files on it.
He begins typing.
Bulgakov sits on the other chair. He stares vacantly. Ignores the paperwork on the table.
Stalin pauses.

Stalin What's up?

Bulgakov says nothing.

Trouble at home?

The slightest of nods from Bulgakov confirms. Stalin sighs. He stands up and walks round to sit with Bulgakov.

Terrible things happen, Mikhail.

Bulgakov is surprised at the insight.

Yes, in any great revolutionary enterprise, some terrible things will happen. And if you want to walk away now, I would understand. I wouldn't hold it against you. But . . . I tell you this – the worst is over, the hard work is done.

He's up on his feet now, warming to his theme.

For both of us. Look where I've got to – he's in prison, but he's telling the guards what to do. It's easy – from here on in, it practically writes itself. And look –

He indicates the administrative files.

The nation is industrialised, the peasants are . . . aligned to the path of true socialism. The storm is no longer raging and the sea is calm. From here on in, the country practically governs itself. We're a boring, modern, progressive state. No more mountains to climb, no more canyons to cross, no more . . . no more terrible things.

He lets it all sink in.

Still, if you want to walk away, I'd understand.

It's Bulgakov's turn to get to his feet.
He paces around.

Bulgakov I'm sorry . . . I just don't think I'm . . .

But the script in the typewriter catches his eye.

He's in prison?

Stalin Yes.

Bulgakov But he tells the guards what to do?

Stalin Yes.

Bulgakov The man is trapped but his soul is still free.

Stalin That's what I was trying to imply –

Bulgakov It's good. But what if one day the governor orders the guards to punish him? Really hurt him.

Stalin Yes . . . He walks between them –

Bulgakov – and they're all hitting him with sticks –

Stalin – one after the other –

Bulgakov – but he doesn't flinch!

Stalin Like Christ on the way to Calvary! Or is that too much?

Bulgakov Put it in anyway.

Stalin Put it in anyway!

Stalin returns to his desk. He starts typing urgently.

Typing with a flourish.
Bulgakov watches him for a moment, then follows his example. He sits down to his collection of paperwork. He signs documents, one after another, working his way briskly through the pile.
Both work fast. Until:

Bulgakov Stop!

Stalin What's wrong?

Bulgakov Have you seen these?

Stalin Seen what?

Bulgakov Confessions. Signed confessions.

Stalin Really? Who from?

Bulgakov From . . . Zinoviev . . . Kamenev . . . Nikolai Bukharin.

Stalin Kamenev – he and I go way back. I knew him when he was plain old Lev Rosenfeld. Nikolai Bukharin – the smartest guy in the Party by a long way. And Zinoviev? – that man was trusted by Lenin himself. You can't fault those men. They were there at the Revolution. So what've they done? Filched the petty cash? Double-dipped on expenses? Impregnated a ballerina? Boys will be boys, Mikhail.

Bulgakov They plotted against you.

Stalin No!

Bulgakov That's what they've confessed to.

Stalin Three of my very, very best friends and you sit there and tell me they're plotting against me!

Bulgakov It's just what's written here –

Stalin is distraught. He walks around.
Takes a confession and reads it.

Stalin This is absurd. If these confessions were true, it would mean that the entire Revolution was nothing more than a front for a long-term Trotskyite-bourgeois plot.

Bulgakov You're right.

Stalin As far as I'm concerned, those men are innocent. These so called confessions are merely evidence of someone else's mischief.

He returns to the desk.
Hesitates.

And yet . . .

Bulgakov What?

Stalin Nothing.

Bulgakov You're worried.

Stalin No!

Bulgakov What is it?

Stalin Well . . . they signed them.

Bulgakov Yes, but that doesn't mean –

Stalin They signed them!

Bulgakov Joseph – you said yourself – it's impossible. They cannot be true. There is nothing to worry about.

Stalin Oh God, I feel sick. The betrayal!

Bulgakov Calm down. Please. Perhaps it's all a misunderstanding.

Stalin Misunderstanding! Confessing to conspiracy to murder me, disband the Party, and install the puppet leader of a combined Anglo-German military dictatorship. What scale of misunderstanding are we talking about here?

Bulgakov Well – you know – someone said something to someone else who said something else to someone else that got taken out of context and overheard and then someone else said something and . . . you can imagine it all ends up in a mess. And then you get these! Worthless. Nothing.

Stalin You think so?

Bulgakov Yes.

Stalin You're not just saying that to make me feel better?

Bulgakov You've known these men for years.

Stalin Yes.

Bulgakov Three of your very, very best friends.

Stalin Yes.

Bulgakov So, if you ask me, they're obviously innocent. But – for everyone's peace of mind, not least yours – it's not going to hurt to make a few, simple enquiries?

Stalin A few . . . simple enquiries. No, you're right. That's not going to hurt, is it?

Bulgakov No. Not hurt anyone. So let's stay calm.

Stalin Yes. Calm.

A beat.

They signed them!

Bulgakov Joseph! . . . Calm.

Stalin obeys.

Now watch.

He takes a pen and scribbles in the margin of one of the confessions.

'Make further enquiries . . . J.S.' That'll sort it all out.

Stalin Mikhail . . . What can I say?

Lost for words, he hugs Bulgakov.
   Then he steps back and picks up the latest
manuscript from the desk.
   He presses it into his hand.
   Exit Stalin.

Bulgakov turns and approaches the bed.
   He sees that it is empty.
   He calls offstage.

Bulgakov Yelena? Yelena! I'm home. Please – come back
to bed.

No reply.
   Enter Vladimir and Stepan.
   Stepan raps on the table as they stride.
   Vladimir is holding a bloodstained handkerchief to
his cheek.

Vladimir Bulgakov!

Bulgakov Vladimir – what the hell do you want?

Vladimir We need your car!

Bulgakov What?

Vladimir Your car. Now.

Bulgakov Are you all right?

Vladimir What? This – shaving, that's all. Listen, your
driver will accept orders only from you, so please – we
need you to come with us.

Bulgakov So where are we going?

Vladimir To make an arrest.

Bulgakov An arrest! Who?

Vladimir consults a list.

Vladimir I don't know. Some loser. We've been up all night. About one in the morning. The phone rings. It's my boss, screaming at me. 'Someone's been plotting against Stalin. Get out there. Make further enquiries.' So we've been all over town, begging rides from one place to another. How do they expect us to arrest people – without a car? What way is that to run an organ of state security?

Bulgakov You're right. It's ridiculous.

A beat.

Vladimir You got the scene?

Bulgakov Yes. Of course.

He delves into his coat.

Vladimir Gimme.

Bulgakov hands over the latest instalment.
He watches Vladimir skim through it. Still dabbing at the cut.

Bulgakov You weren't shaving.

Vladimir Some women get upset when they think they're never going to see their husbands again. Not that mine would complain! This is good. I like it. He's in prison. But they can't break him. In fact he converts the guards to Marxism! I love it!

Stepan hurries offstage.
He returns with a Man and Woman in their nightclothes, both in handcuffs.
Vladimir consults a list.

Am I right? You are the General Secretary of the Turkmenistan All-Union Communist Party?

Man Yes, I am.

Vladimir And you are his wife?

Woman Yes.

Vladimir In town for the congress?

Man Yes. That's correct.

Vladimir You have a return ticket to Turkmenistan?

Man Yes.

He produces it from his pocket and Vladimir snatches it away.

Vladimir You may claim a refund, Comrade.

Man What have I done?

Vladimir Conspiracy to assassinate Stalin, wreck the economy, overthrow the government, restore the Tsar. And so forth.

Man Please – I'll confess. To anything. But let my wife go. Please.

Vladimir Shut up.

Man Please, let her go!

Stepan punches the Man once in the stomach. The Man sinks to his knees.
Bulgakov pulls Vladimir aside.

Bulgakov Vladimir! That man is an old Bolshevik! He probably stormed the Winter Palace.

Vladimir So?

Bulgakov He doesn't seem a very likely traitor.

Vladimir Oh, how naive you are. Listen, Mikhail: a man may appear innocent. He may even be 'innocent' as the term is conventionally understood. But he will have what we call objective characteristics which clearly point the other way.

79

Bulgakov Objective characteristics?

Vladimir In this case: that he is in a position of power.

Bulgakov And that's enough to make him a potential traitor, is it?

Vladimir More than enough.

Bulgakov His wife? What about her?

Vladimir She has the objective characteristic of being his wife.

The Woman turns to Bulgakov.

Woman Please, Comrade – tell your men – we have done nothing wrong. We are good citizens.

Vladimir That's how it works when you make enquiries.

Vladimir and Stepan exit with the Man and Woman.
Bulgakov is alone on the stage.
Enter the two Actors.
Actor One is in prison uniform.
Actor Two wears a police hat and jacket.

Actor Two Dzughashvili! You have corrupted too many guards to your treacherous ideology!

Actor One So what? Are you going to beat me? I do not care. You can never break me!

Actor Two No – we are sending you to Siberia and from there you will never come back! Ha ha ha!

Exit Actor Two.
Enter Grigory stage right.

Grigory Mikhail!

Bulgakov Grigory – what are you doing out here?

Grigory Looking for you.

Bulgakov For me?

Grigory I need your help.

Bulgakov Tell me – anything I can do –

Grigory My work is banned now. I'm banned! Everything I've ever written and everything I ever write in the future.

Bulgakov Oh Christ.

Grigory Unless I give in – unless I deliver a suitably damning self-criticism.

Bulgakov Grigory –

Grigory I refused. So I'm allowed to go on breathing, but that's it, that's the limit of my permissible creative activity. They buried me alive, Mikhail.

Bulgakov I'm sorry.

Grigory Can you help me?

Bulgakov hugs Grigory.
Exit Grigory.

Actor One They can send me to Siberia, but they will never break me. I am not Dzughashvili any more. I am Stalin!

Exit Actor One.
Bulgakov turns back towards the table, cupboard, etc.

Bulgakov Hello? Hello? Anyone home?

No one. Then he has a idea.
He slides open the cupboard.

Sergei – will you come out?

Sergei emerges cautiously.

Where is everyone?

Sergei Mrs Bulgakov – she has gone out – distributing food.

Bulgakov Oh. Well, that's fine. That's all right. We have plenty.

Sergei And Vasilly and Praskovya – they both went to work yesterday – but they never came back.

Bulgakov Never came back?

Sergei No.

Bulgakov What does that mean?

Sergei I don't know. They didn't come back.

Bulgakov How strange. Not like them at all. Still, they'll be back soon. I'm sure.

Sergei Mr Bulgakov – can I tell you about something? It happened at work.

Bulgakov Of course.

Sergei The manager of the factory. He couldn't meet the targets. It wasn't his fault. We worked hard, extra shifts – so did he. But it still wasn't enough. So he lied. Claimed we had made more tractors than we really had. It was the wrong thing to do, but . . . He was found out, of course. They were coming to arrest him but he committed suicide.

Bulgakov I see.

Sergei What do you think of that?

Bulgakov Well, it's obviously a tragedy, for the man and his family.

Sergei They said he was a wrecker, a saboteur, and that's why the targets weren't being met.

Bulgakov Yes . . . Well . . . I suppose, you have to look at it from the point of view of the authorities. Clearly this man had . . . objective characteristics. That's what it is. That's why he was under suspicion. That's how enquiries work. Of course, there's no way that I could have known that.

Sergei I'm sorry, Comrade, I do not have your education –

Bulgakov Of course. You see, a man may appear innocent, but his position, of power and responsibility, means that he must inevitably be suspect. Think about it: the factory fails to meet its targets, he lies, and then he commits suicide before he can be arrested. Possibly to protect someone else. You put it all together . . .

Sergei He left a note on his desk, denouncing the whole system.

Bulgakov Well, that fits in, doesn't it? Don't you think so? It has to, doesn't it?

Sergei Like Praskovya and Vasilly, then?

Bulgakov What about them?

Sergei They have objective characteristics too, I think.

Bulgakov No.

Sergei He was a landowner. A possible Tsarist?

Bulgakov Vasilly is harmless.

Sergei And she teaches history – perhaps she subverts through counter-revolutionary propaganda.

Bulgakov That's not necessarily how it will be taken. There is, I'm sure, a perfectly innocent explanation for their absence.

Silence.

Sergei The suicide note – left by my boss – when the police came, they arrested anyone who had read it.

Bulgakov That's just a precaution. That's all.

A beat.

You didn't read the note, did you, Sergei?

Sergei stares at Bulgakov. Turns away.
The sound of a knock at the door.
Sergei scuttles into his cupboard and pulls it fast.
Enter the Driver.

Driver Your car is ready, sir.

Bulgakov Thank you – I'll be out in a moment.

Exit the Driver.

Sergei.

No response.
Enter Yelena.
They both stop and look at one another.
A frosty silence from Yelena.
Bulgakov moves as though everything is normal.

Bulgakov Did the food go down well?

Yelena says nothing.

Yelena –

Yelena Men and women are being arrested, for nothing at all. Every morning, another apartment is empty. And the first question they are asked is: who is in this conspiracy with you?

Bulgakov has no reply.
Yelena walks across to the gramophone.
She places a record on, winds it up, and drops the stylus in place.
It is their tune.
She looks at her husband. He cannot meet her gaze.
He turns away.

The music plays.
Yelena turns and walks away. She exits.
Bulgakov stands alone.
The music plays on.
After a while, it sticks.
The needle jumps, over and over.
Bulgakov walks across to the gramophone.
He lifts the stylus. Removes the record.

Enter the two Actors. They busy themselves with their sack of props and costumes.
Vladimir and Stepan follow as before.
Bulgakov approaches.

Vladimir I'm being followed.

Bulgakov Isn't everyone?

Vladimir Of course, that's normal – but now I'm really being followed.

Bulgakov Is there a difference?

Vladimir Yes – of course there is! It's . . . You wouldn't understand.

Bulgakov I don't.

Vladimir You've changed.

Bulgakov Have I?

Vladimir That man we arrested. Do you think he was guilty?

Bulgakov You said he was.

Vladimir Forget what I said.

Bulgakov He had objective characteristics.

Vladimir Forget them. Do you think he was guilty?

Bulgakov He confessed, didn't he?

Vladimir He confessed. Yes. To Stepan.

Bulgakov Well, there you are.

Vladimir So did his wife.

A beat.

There we are.

A beat.

How do you feel about the play? About your play?

Bulgakov What does it matter what I think of it? If I like it or don't like it, so what? I'm doing it so that my play *Molière* can be performed again.

Vladimir I want your critical assessment.

Bulgakov All right. It's a . . . solid, if unflashy piece of drama. An effective account of . . .

Vladimir Bullshit! You expect me to believe that? From the man who wrote *The White Guard*, you're telling me that's your opinion on this?

Bulgakov remains silent.

You've convinced yourself, have you? Of what else have you convinced yourself?

Bulgakov I still stand opposed to everything you represent.

Vladimir Sure you do.

A pause.
    Vladimir stares at him.
    Bulgakov breaks it off.
    He walks away. Sits down at the table.
    Exit Vladimir, Stepan, the two Actors.
    Bulgakov sits alone a moment.

Enter Stalin with a large bundle of files under each arm.
He drops them with a thump on to the desk.

Stalin I'm not happy about this.

Bulgakov About what?

Stalin About what? Well, it only turns out that the entire USSR is riddled with traitors. That within every single institution: the Party, the army, academia, culture, science, industry, and so on – there are millions – yes, millions – of spies, traitors, wreckers, counter-revolutionaries, and Trotskyite capitalist bourgeois Tsarists!

A beat.

And it's all your fault.

Bulgakov My fault!

Stalin 'Make further enquiries.'

Bulgakov What?

Stalin That's what you wrote.

Bulgakov Yes, I did, but –

Stalin – and this is what happens! A conspiracy beyond the human imagination. Your creation, Mikhail!

Bulgakov That's not really fair. I mean, just because my instruction uncovered it – that doesn't make me responsible. Does it?

Stalin I would have let sleeping dogs lie.

Bulgakov But Joseph –

Stalin Each confession leads to another fifty. It's an exponential catastrophe!

Bulgakov I'm sorry! I didn't mean this to happen.

From the stacks of papers, Stalin grabs several at random. Reads from them.

Stalin Consider the following, uncovered only this morning. There are students in Leningrad who plan to assassinate me. An aeronautical engineer in Novosibirsk who designs planes that crash. A Kazakh dairy worker puts nails in the butter, and a vet in the Ukraine poisons twenty million horses. Practically every employee on the trans-Siberian railway spies for Japan. An industrial commissar in Magnitogorsk spends every waking hour orchestrating the production of defective steel. And thousands upon thousands of people freely engage in rootless cosmopolitanism.

Bulgakov Sorry?

Stalin Being Jewish. And spying for Germany.

Bulgakov Is that likely?

Stalin It's possible. Anything is possible. But you know what's scary – what's really scary – is they're all connected.

Bulgakov Are you certain of that?

Stalin You think I'm making it up?

Bulgakov No!

Stalin What am I going to do?

Bulgakov I don't know . . .

Stalin You don't know?

Bulgakov No.

Stalin OK . . . I'll deal with it myself. I'll sift through them, one by one, confession by confession, network by network, step by step, for as long as it takes, because – you understand, of course – there's no one else I can trust. I'll do this. You finish the play.

He swivels the typewriter round so that it faces Bulgakov.

Now Stalin starts work. He snatches at sheets of paper from the stacks of files.

Scrawls in the margins, cross-references, compares, places the sheets in new piles, rearranges, etc.

While doing so, he mutters to himself.

After a little while, he notices that Bulgakov has not moved at all.

I'd get a move on, if I was you, Mikhail. Time is running out. The play has to be ready for the twenty-first. And of course, if there's no play, there's no deal. No deal, no *Molière*. No *Molière*, no future. No point to anything. Is there?

Bulgakov I can't.

Stalin Of course you can.

Bulgakov I can't.

Stalin But you're the talented playwright! You're the man who wrote *The White Guard*!

Bulgakov watches Stalin absorbed in his task.

Bulgakov I can't write this. I never could. I need your help.

Stalin Sorry! Busy! Big conspiracy!

He continues, muttering and whistling to himself.

Bulgakov Joseph . . . Please . . .

No response.

(*Eventually.*) General Secretary, you need a system.

Stalin stops immediately.

Stalin A what?

Bulgakov A system.

Stalin A system! Of course! So what's that for?

Bulgakov To make the process logical. You see, at the moment, you've got all these confessions – it's overwhelming. But if the conspiracy exists –

Stalin Which it does –

Bulgakov Yes – and the resources to deal with it –

Stalin – are inherently undermined by the conspiracy itself.

Bulgakov Yes . . . Then the key is to say: right, let's solve so many cases, out of the total.

Stalin A quota?

Bulgakov Yes, a quota of cases to be resolved. Concentrate on these, break the links, what's left is nothing. These individuals – students, engineers, politicians, rootless . . . whatever – on their own – harmless.

Stalin The individuals don't matter?

Bulgakov In a manner of speaking.

Stalin thinks it over.
He gathers up all his loose sheets of paper. He taps them together and drops them on top of one of the stacks of files.
He smiles.

Stalin You see. It wasn't so difficult after all. Not for a clever guy like you. 'A system,' he says. A system! The simplicity! The genius. You may . . .

He twirls a finger towards the typewriter.
Bulgakov swivels it back round towards Stalin.

Thank you.

He begins typing.

Only friends can do that. Men who respect each other.

He types some more, then pauses.

Is there anything that I can do for you?

Bulgakov Well, actually, there is. It's a favour for me, well – for a friend.

Stalin The young writer?

Bulgakov Yes.

Stalin Having trouble? Some over-zealous, nit-picking bureaucrat doesn't know talent when he sees it?

Bulgakov That's right.

Stalin Consider it dealt with. From now on – every word that young man writes is to be published.

Bulgakov Thanks. That'll mean a lot to him.

Stalin It's the least I can do. I owe you so much. And what's more, Mikhail, I've enjoyed it.

*He holds out the customary large envelope of script.
Bulgakov takes the envelope.*

Bulgakov Thanks.

*Bulgakov walks away.
Stalin puts the unlit pipe in his mouth.
Exit Stalin.*

*Enter Yelena and Anna.
They are at the table as Bulgakov approaches.*

Sorry to – I've been working all night. Coffee?

Anna How's it going?

Bulgakov Fine. I mean it's nearly finished.

91

Anna Is it good?

Bulgakov Not for me to say. The audience will decide. They always do.

Anna Surely you have a view.

Bulgakov I think it's too early to say.

Anna Is there anything you do have a view on any more, Mikhail?

Bulgakov What is this? Yelena?

Yelena Anna has something to tell you.

Anna They have destroyed him.

Bulgakov What? Grigory? No – it's all right. I have it on good authority – he's going to be unbanned. Rehabilitated. They're going to review his previous work, but from now on, anything he writes – anything – is guaranteed publication. Guaranteed!

Anna He's written this.

She holds a single sheet of paper, typed on one side.

Bulgakov What's that?

Enter Grigory. He stands apart.

Anna 'I have failed in my most basic duty to support the Revolution. I have created works that glorify the bourgeois and deny the rightful role of the proletariat. I have betrayed the faith of the people and it is only fitting that my work should cease to be published or read.' What do you think this is?

Bulgakov It's his self-criticism. I told him not to write it. In any case, the situation has been resolved –

Anna Oh yes, it certainly has. This is more than a critique.

Bulgakov is silent.
He approaches Anna and takes the note.

Grigory 'Like a parasite upon the body of the nation, I have sucked nourishment but given nothing in return. I have distorted truth, corrupted minds, and incited counter-revolution. My guilt is no less for my confession and I accept my punishment as both fitting and lenient.'

Grigory produces a revolver.

Bulgakov Oh, God. No.

Grigory shoots himself. Falls dead to the floor.

Anna Publish anything he writes from now on. That's a funny joke. Grigory would have liked it. He always said your greatest talent was for comedy.

Anna stands up and exits.
The two Actors enter to remove Grigory's body.
Bulgakov and Yelena are alone now.

Yelena Sergei's gone.

Bulgakov says nothing.

He went out, to work.

Bulgakov And never came back.

Yelena No.

Bulgakov How strange it all is.

A beat.

Yelena Mikhail, what have you done?

She exits.

Enter Stalin.
Stalin sits, typing and laughing.
Bulgakov sits. He does nothing.

Stalin stops. Looks up.
He gets up and pours a vodka for Bulgakov.
He places a slim file on the desk in front of
Bulgakov.
He returns to his seat and resumes typing.
Bulgakov's gaze falls on the slim file.
His attention grows. He takes the top sheet and
studies it intently.

Stalin Now what do you think of this? We're in the private apartments of Tsar Nicholas the Second. He's got this canary that sings the national anthem. That's sort of a metaphor – you think it's too heavy-handed? Brainless bird in cage sings national anthem? Anyway, I like it for now – we can take it out later if we don't like it –

Bulgakov What is this!

Stalin stops. Puts down his manuscript.
He walks around and takes a look at the page in
Bulgakov's hand.

Stalin Mass-operational order double-zero double-four seven. It estimates the number of potential traitors, wreckers, counter-revolutionaries and so forth, in each and every area of the entire Soviet Union.

Bulgakov And what are these numbers?

Stalin Second category is the number to go to the camps.

Bulgakov And the first?

Stalin That's the number to be . . . you know . . . shot.

Bulgakov Killed?

Stalin If it works properly. A quota –

Bulgakov Of people to be shot.

Stalin It was your idea.

Bulgakov My idea!

Stalin You said I need a system –

Bulgakov Not like this!

Stalin A quota of cases to be resolved. It's true, Mikhail, you are a genius. At one stroke you removed the guesswork, the random nature of it all. Your inspiration has replaced it with a system that is understandable, reproducible and above all – effective. Now sign here.

Bulgakov Quotas of people to be shot.

Stalin It's the only fair way to do it.

Bulgakov Fair?

Stalin Any attempt to separate the guilty from the innocent is going to take for ever. And who's to say it even works? This way, it's over, it's done, the problem is solved and we can all move on with our lives. You included.

Bulgakov We're talking about human beings!

Stalin No, no, no. That's where you're wrong! That's the beauty of it. With your system –

Bulgakov It's not my system!

Stalin – all we're dealing with is numbers.

Bulgakov Each number is an individual.

Stalin But the individuals don't matter. Do they? Just sign it there for me, Mikhail, and the rest.

Bulgakov is stunned. He walks away, holding the order.

Anyway, two of the Tsar's ministers come in – and the canary keeps breaking into the national anthem, and every time it does, they have to stand up and sing and then sit down – you can imagine – it could be really funny. I can take it out if it doesn't work. So, these two ministers are there to tell the Tsar about the demonstrations in Georgia. And they tell the Tsar about this rebel leader: Stalin. The Tsar says: 'Stalin – who's he? No one!' Wrong! Then he asks how many of the demonstrators were killed. 'Fourteen,' says the flunky. 'Fourteen!' says the Tsar. 'Court-martial the commanding officer! A whole battalion of cossacks against six thousand demonstrators and only fourteen dead – that's outrageous!'

Stalin laughs.
But no response from Bulgakov.

It's satire.

Bulgakov I want it to stop.

Stalin The satire?

Bulgakov The investigations!

Stalin Who got out of bed the wrong side this morning?

Bulgakov The further enquiries! The whole process! It's gone too far!

He wields the operational order.

This is obscene.

Stalin No, Mikhail, this is finishing the job.

Bulgakov I will not collaborate with this.

Stalin But I love it when you collaborate.

Bulgakov No!

Stalin Haven't I been good to you? Hasn't our relationship been good for you? I've done your work . . .

Bulgakov No! I won't do it. These are not numbers. These are people. This has got to stop!

He thumps the desk.
A stand-off.
For a moment, it seems Stalin might turn nasty.

Stalin It's got to stop?

Bulgakov I . . . demand . . . I demand that you stop it.
Now.

Stalin takes this in.

Stalin Well, I've always admired a man who's true to his
principles. It takes one to know one. And I've always
looked up to you – your number-one fan, remember?
Besides, I'm just the son of a cobbler from Gori, whereas
you – university-educated, a writer – who am I to tell
you what to do? Mikhail, if you say it's got to stop, it's
got to stop.

Bulgakov Really?

Stalin Yes.

He takes out the scene he has just typed from the
typewriter. Places it in an envelope.

Consider it stopped. It was a just an idea. A crazy idea.
But you're probably right. You usually are.

Bulgakov No signatures?

Stalin No!

Bulgakov No quotas for arrest and execution?

Stalin No. I promise.

Pause.

Now let's talk about the play.

But Bulgakov is still withdrawn, trembling.

Please. Come on, Mikhail. The play.

Bulgakov Sorry, I don't feel in the mood.

Stalin You're still upset. I can see that. About these . . . But can't we just forget about all that? Let's not let it spoil things. Oh God, I wish I'd never . . . I admit it: quotas, mass executions – the whole idea was a mistake. I'm sorry. I thought you'd like it. I thought you'd approve. I'm sorry. Please.

He extends a hand.
A reluctant reciprocation.
They shake.

Vodka?

Bulgakov I have to go.

Stalin All right. Sure. Till next time.

Bulgakov turns to go.

Hey! Don't forget this. The reason you're here.

He holds out the envelope.
Bulgakov takes it.
Exit Stalin.

Bulgakov turns back towards the bed.
Yelena enters.
They stare at each other for a beat.
She's wary. Angry.
He sits on the bed. He holds out the envelope.
She makes no move to take it.

Bulgakov I told myself I could do this. I could find a way to give them what they wanted and still be myself.

He offers out the envelope again.
Yelena approaches.
She takes the envelope and takes out the few pages of manuscript.
She reads them quickly.

She sighs. Returns the pages to the envelope. Hands them back to Bulgakov.

It's as bad as that?

Yelena sits on the bed. She says nothing.

I knew I could rely on you. Should have asked you sooner.

Pause.

I want to leave this country now. Will you come with me, Yelena?

Yelena Yes.

Bulgakov Do you still have the tickets to Leningrad?

Yelena Yes. And the currency and the false papers and the letter to Anna's cousin who will lead us across the ice. I have it all, Mikhail. All I have been waiting for is you.

He takes her hand.
  They sit for a moment.
  She exits.

Enter the two Actors, Vladimir and Stepan.
  Bulgakov approaches.
  He hands over the envelope.
  Vladimir takes out the typed pages and skim-reads.

Vladimir Fine. Funny. Great. Only one scene left to write.

Bulgakov No. That's the end. That's the final scene.

Vladimir No, it is not the end, Bulgakov. I'm the director of this play and I'm telling you we're one scene short.

Bulgakov I'm finished.

Vladimir But the play is not! Tomorrow is his birthday, and for tonight I have scheduled a full dress rehearsal and I want – I demand! – one more scene!

Bulgakov I'm having nothing more to do with this.

Vladimir It's your play.

Bulgakov No, it's not and it never will be!

Vladimir It's started, you know.

Bulgakov What has?

Vladimir Do you know what's happened? He's issued mass-operation orders. They identify the numbers – the quotas –

Bulgakov To be arrested and shot.

Vladimir All across the Soviet Union.

Bulgakov I know. But it's all right. You see, I didn't sign them.

Vladimir What?

Bulgakov The operational orders – I didn't sign them. I refused.

Vladimir What are you talking about? These are orders from the Politburo, from Joseph Stalin himself. They don't need the signature of some fucking writer.

Bulgakov But I didn't –

Vladimir Listen. An avalanche of terror is about to descend upon us, upon this country. Everything you've witnessed so far, everything you've heard about, has just been a warm-up. And in honour of that, I want you to write one more scene, Mikhail. One scene, where you get inside his head, where you reveal exactly what makes him the bastard he is. That will be our gift to posterity – the truth. And after that, well, we're probably fucked anyway.

Bulgakov No. I'm sorry, Vladimir. I quit.

Exit Bulgakov.
Vladimir watches him go. Turns to his cast.

Vladimir All right! On your feet. Let's get ready!

Exit all as Bulgakov enters.
He stops at the table. Exhausted. Supports himself on it.
He retches. He is weak.
A spasm of abdominal pain. He moves on.
He goes to the bed.

Bulgakov Yelena? Yelena!

No reply.
He starts to undress, but is too weak to continue.
He collapses back on the bed.
Moonlight on the bed.
Silence for a few moments.
Then a knocking from within the cupboard.
Bulgakov manages to sit up.
The knocking continues.
Bulgakov staggers up from the bed.
He searches for the source of the noise.
He realises: the knocking comes from within the cupboard.
He approaches. Stands in front of the door.
With a final thump, the knocking stops.
Cautiously, Bulgakov raises a hand to the door.
And suddenly it slides violently open.
The backlit silhouetted figure inside lets out a yell.
Bulgakov jumps back with a shriek.
The music starts.
Stalin pounces towards Bulgakov.
Bulgakov flees, but he is weak.
Stalin toys with his prey like a cat with a wounded bird.
Finally, he chooses the moment to catch him.

He throws Bulgakov to the floor.

Stalin Bulgakov – I feel hurt! Angry! And do you know why? Because I hear they want another scene. Is that true? One more scene – written by you and you alone – one that will expose me for what I really am? You know what I think of that?

Bulgakov retches.

Well –

He breaks into a smile.

I love it! The truth! What a great idea! What a crazy wonderful idea! And no one, Mikhail, no one is more qualified to write the truth than you.

He hauls Bulgakov up and pushes him into a seat at the desk in front of the typewriter.

You can't walk away from this, Mikhail. It's in your blood. One more scene. And I can't do it for you this time. Only you can do it, only you can get inside my head. That's a privilege, and a burden, perhaps. But it's your destiny and you can't lie there sleeping while it waits for you.

A beat. Bulgakov is weak, helpless. Stalin gestures with his pipe.

Put the paper in, Mikhail.

Bulgakov obeys.

Now I'd love to stay and watch the creative process, but my car is waiting. You know how it is – busy, busy, busy. Those mass-operation orders – my turn to confess: I signed them anyway. I forged your forgery of my signature. Hope you don't mind. Seemed to work: we're putting them into action! Operational Order double-zero double-four seven goes live at 02.00 hours. It's going to be quite a show. Like yours, Mikhail. Keep an eye on the time. You wouldn't want to miss your train.

Exit Stalin back into the cupboard. The door slides shut.

Bulgakov sits and stares at the blank page in front of him.

Enter the Cleaner with mop, bucket and folded tarpaulin.

She unfolds the tarpaulin on the floor.

She begins to mop it, slow and rhythmic.

Enter Vladimir, Stepan and the two Actors.

Vladimir Dress rehearsal. From the top.

The Actors perform, swiftly changing hats, costumes etc., every couple of lines.

Actor One A bishop!

Actor Two A cobbler.

Actor One A leader of men!

Actor Two Welcome to the seminary.

Actor One But I do not believe in God.

Tentatively, Bulgakov raises his hands and begins to stab at the keys.

Actor Two Have you got what it takes to lead?

Actor One Have you got what it takes to follow?

Actor Two Dzughashvili is our hero!

Actor One I am but a humble disciple of Lenin.

Actor Two But now he has been betrayed!

Actor One In Siberia, only the strongest survive.

Actor Two Joseph, my darling, you have come back.

Actor One Yes, but revolution is my true love.

The Cleaner finishes.
She folds up the tarpaulin and carries it off as she exits.
Bulgakov finishes.
He pulls out the final sheet and places it down on top of the others.

Actor Two Joseph, I am ill now. I need a man to succeed me, I need a man to take the revolution forward, to fulfil its promise, to create a true dictatorship of the proletariat. I believe you are that man. Joseph, will you do it for me?

Actor One I will. For the peoples of the Soviet Union – I will!

Exit Actors.
Vladimir contemplates his production in silence.
Behind him Stepan rises to his feet, slowly clapping, a smile on his face.
Exit Vladimir.

Stepan remains on stage.
Dawn light for Bulgakov.
He looks around.

Bulgakov Yelena? My God!

He pulls on his coat.
Exit Bulgakov.

(*Offstage.*) Yelena!

Enter Bulgakov. He looks around.

Vladimir! Vladimir!

He turns to find that he is facing Stepan.

Where is Vladimir?

Stepan says nothing.

I'm looking for my wife. She's been arrested. I need to know where she is. I need to talk to Vladimir.

Stepan Vladimir is dead.

Bulgakov What?

Stepan He was a counter-revolutionary traitor. Did you know that? He mentioned your name under interrogation. Executing him was my first task after I was promoted to replace him. I have his apartment too. And his car. And his wife. We have an arrangement. I fuck her. She lives. Pretty good arrangement, huh?

Bulgakov Where is Yelena?

Stepan Somewhere. In the system. In the meat-grinder. What do I care? Now Vladimir said you weren't quite finished – he was hoping for one more scene.

He snaps his fingers, demanding.

Bulgakov I want to find my wife.

Stepan draws a pistol and aims it at Bulgakov.

Stepan Hand it over.

Bulgakov hands over the folded pages.
Stepan puts the gun away.
He browses through the pages.

Very good. Looks to me like you got right inside his head with this one. The truth!

He lifts something else from his pocket.

Shame the world isn't quite ready for that.

He flicks on the cigarette lighter. He touches it to the edge of the pages, then drops them and watches as they turn to ash.

And to think some people say that manuscripts don't burn.

He stamps on the embers.

Now you, Bulgakov, now it's your turn. You're under arrest.

He approaches Bulgakov to take his arm.
  But Bulgakov snaps.
  Suddenly he is all fury and violence.

Bulgakov No!

He pushes Stepan away. Stepan rushes back at him.
  They fight. Amateur Bulgakov flailing desperately against the tough stocky pro.
  Bulgakov has his hands around Stepan's throat.
  Stepan draws his pistol again.
  Bulgakov releases Stepan's throat, attempts to take hold of the gun.
  They are locked together, wrestling for control of the weapon.
  A single gunshot.
  Both men freeze. Look into each other's eyes.
  Slowly they part.
  Bulgakov looks down. He is holding the gun.
  Stepan looks down in disbelief. He is bleeding from his abdomen.
  He falls to his knees, then slumps to the floor.
  Bulgakov, still holding the gun, looks down at the corpse.
  Sirens.
  Bulgakov walks forward, with the gun in his hand.
  Behind him, the two Actors enter to remove Stepan's body.
  The sirens fade.
  Enter Stalin, carrying a manuscript.
  He places it on the table and sits down.
  Bulgakov turns abruptly, gun in hand aimed at Stalin.

Stalin You don't look so well, Mikhail.

Bulgakov Release my wife.

Stalin 'Or else'?

Bulgakov keeps the gun aimed at Stalin.

What will you achieve if you pull the trigger?

A beat.

You want Yelena to live?

Stalin looks down at the manuscript.

Sign this. Put the gun down. It doesn't suit you. Put it down and sign this.

Bulgakov does not move.

Mikhail, we're not going to get anywhere until you realise that killing will get you nowhere. Put the gun down and sign it.

Bulgakov I'm not signing any more of your orders!

Stalin Oh, no, this isn't my work: it's yours. This is your play, Mikhail. *Young Joseph.*

Bulgakov I didn't write it. It's a piece of shit.

Stalin You're right. A piece of shit. But sign it anyway.

Bulgakov No!

He draws closer with the gun.

Stalin Didn't you wonder: why me? Why you? I'm Joseph Stalin, I could have got whoever I wanted to do whatever I wanted. But it all means so much more when it comes from a man like you.

Bulgakov lowers the gun.

Bulgakov You didn't want a play.

Stalin Not really.

Bulgakov You never did.

Stalin The truth is: it was all about you, Mikhail, all about you from start to finish. Killing my enemies is easy. The challenge is to control their minds. And I think I controlled yours pretty well. In years to come, I'll be able to say: 'Bulgakov? Yeah, we even trained him. We broke him, we can break anybody.' It's man versus monster, Mikhail. And the monster always wins.

> *A beat.*

Yelena can live.

> *Silence. For a long time.*
> *Eventually, Bulgakov places the pistol on the table.*
> *Stalin watches as Bulgakov signs the manuscript.*
> *He turns it to read.*

'*Young Joseph* by Mikhail Bulgakov.'

> *Bulgakov stands back.*

You know, I don't think this will ever be performed. It's served its purpose already.

Bulgakov You never smoke it.

Stalin What?

Bulgakov Your pipe. You hold it but you never light it.

> *Stalin looks at the item in his hand, as though it's the first time he's ever noticed the habit.*

Stalin No. You're right. It's a trick. An illusion.

> *Stalin watches as Bulgakov walks away.*
> *Bulgakov approaches the bed.*
> *Enter Yelena, in white cotton, led on by two*
> *NKVD Men.*
> *Bulgakov sits down on the bed.*